Norman Wei Photography

Birds of the Caribbean
a small sampling

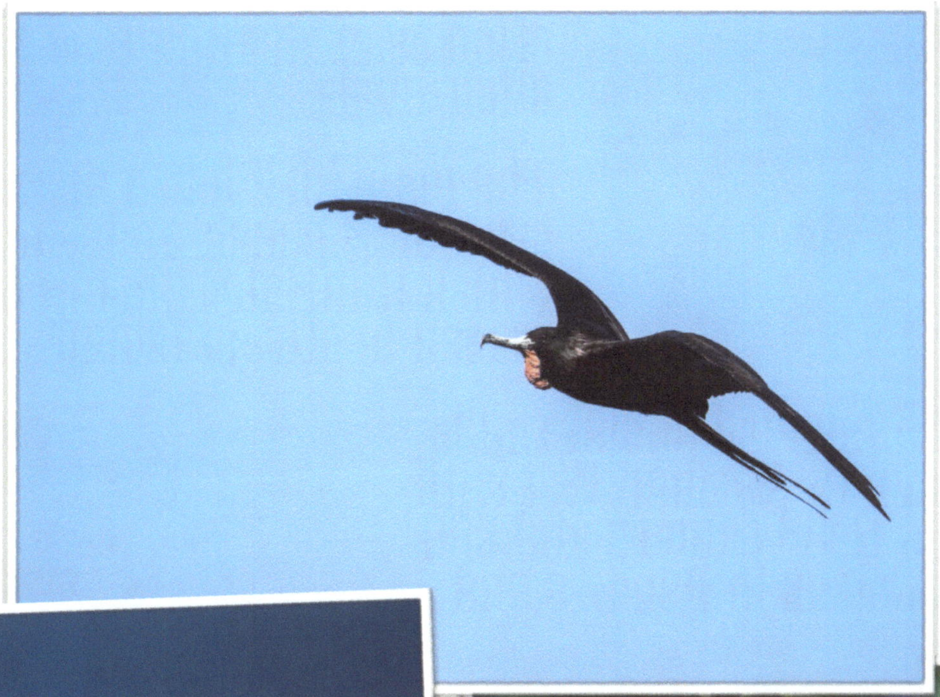

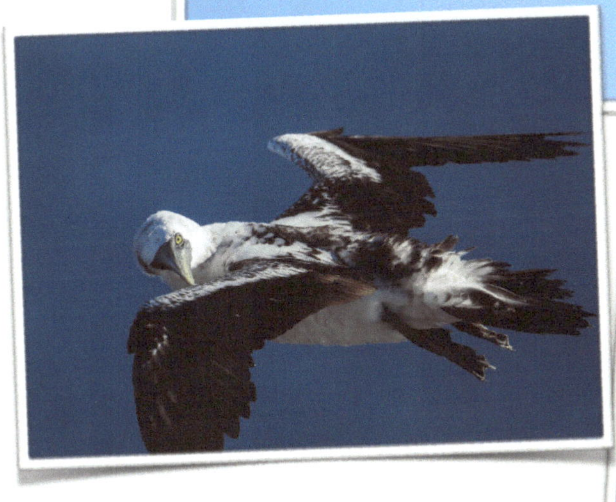

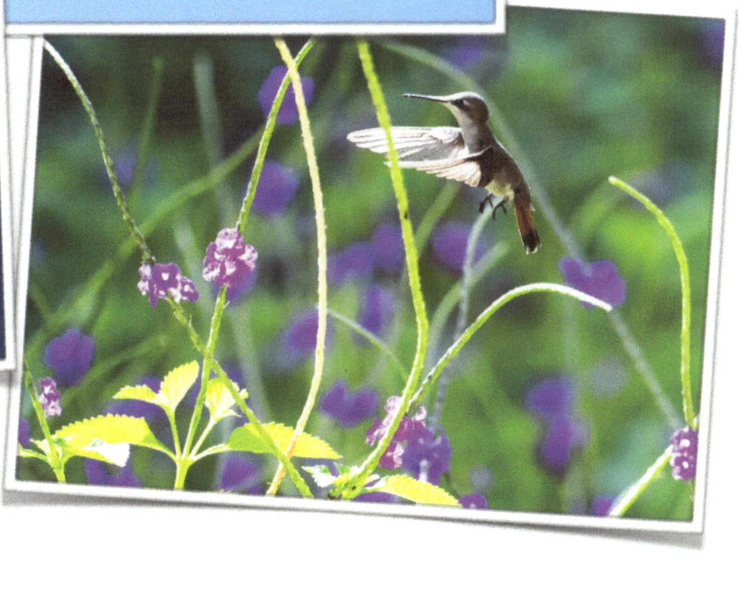

The Magnificent Frigatebird

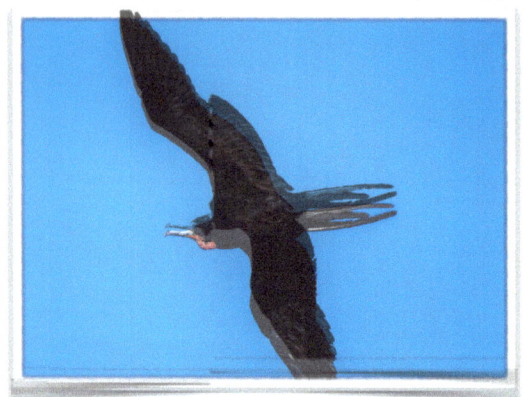

The Magnificent Frigatebird is a tropical sea bird that can stay aloft over the ocean for an extended period of time. It is often seen stealing food from other birds.

The male bird has a distinctive red gulag pouch under its neck which it inflates during mating season to attract females.

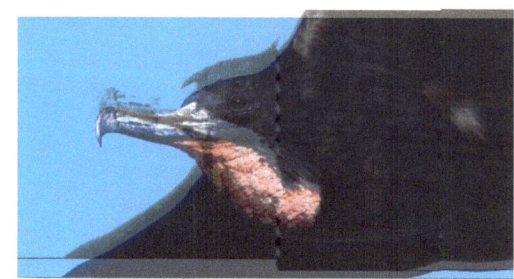

All the frigatebird photographs were taken by Norman Wei with his Nikon D500 camera and 500 mm prime lens in Bonaire and Curacao.

The Magnificent Frigatebird

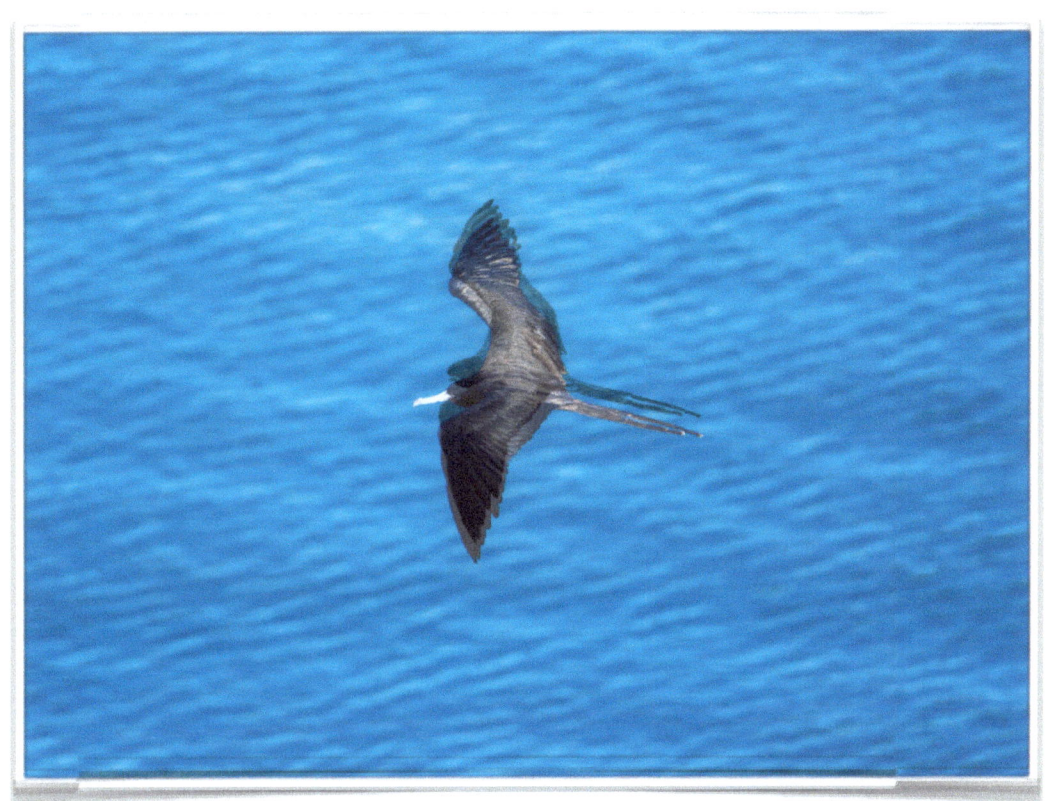

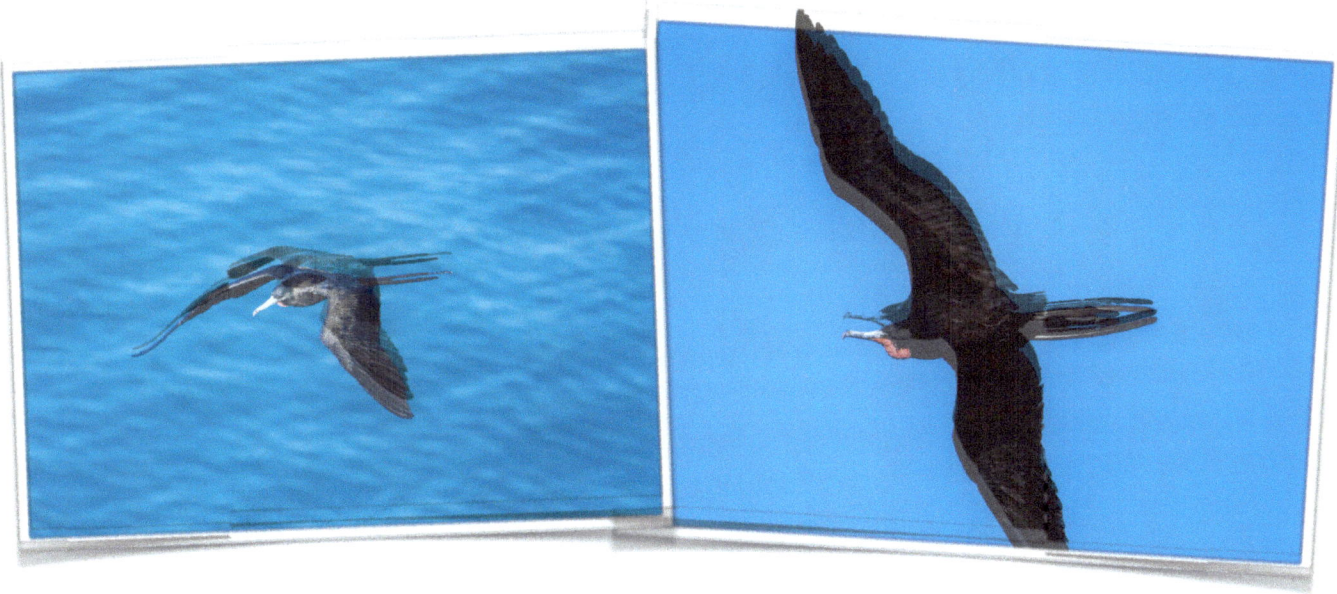

Norman Wei Photography

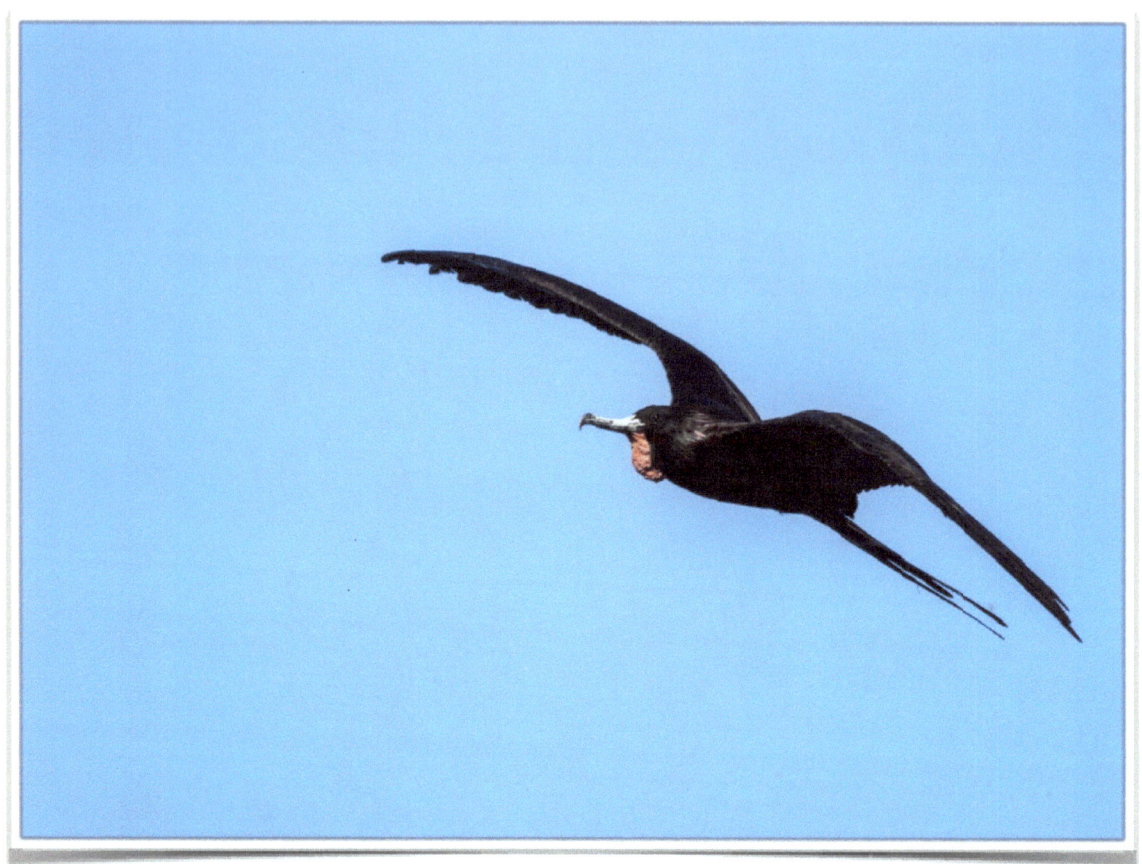

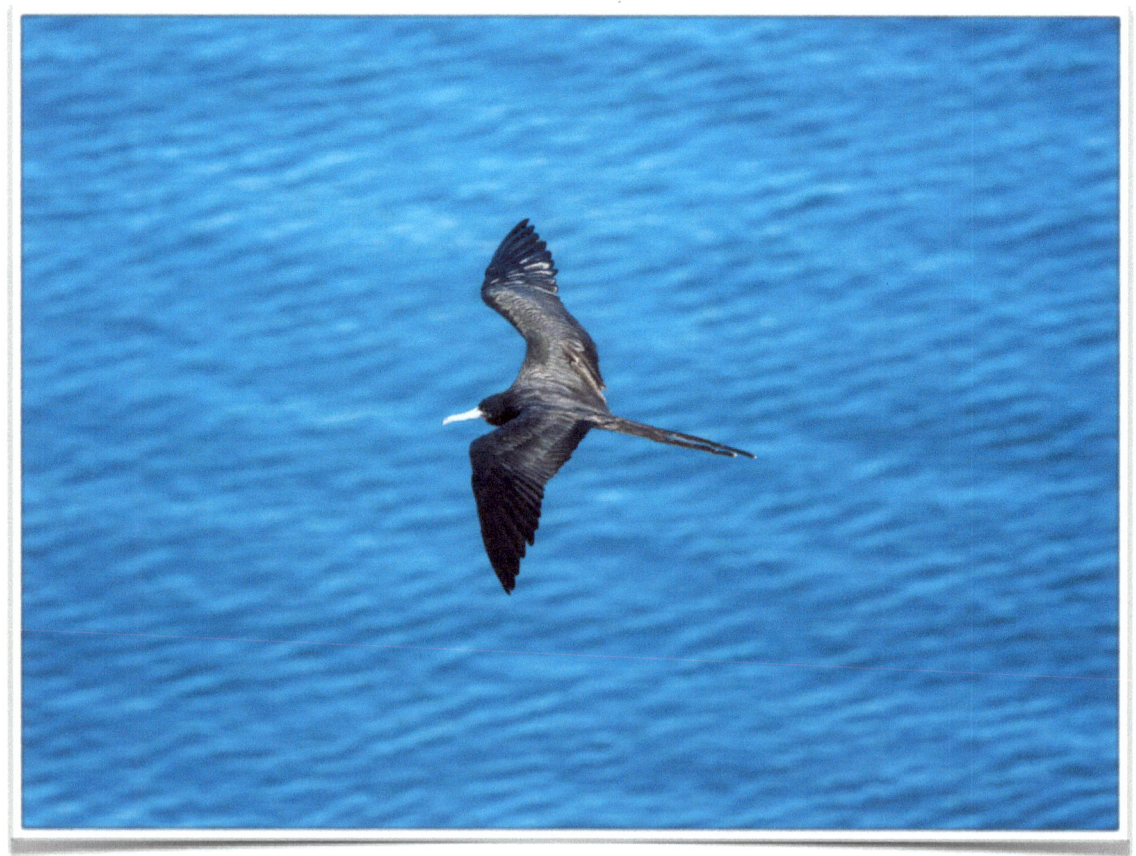

© 2019 Norman Wei Birds of the Caribbean, Page 4

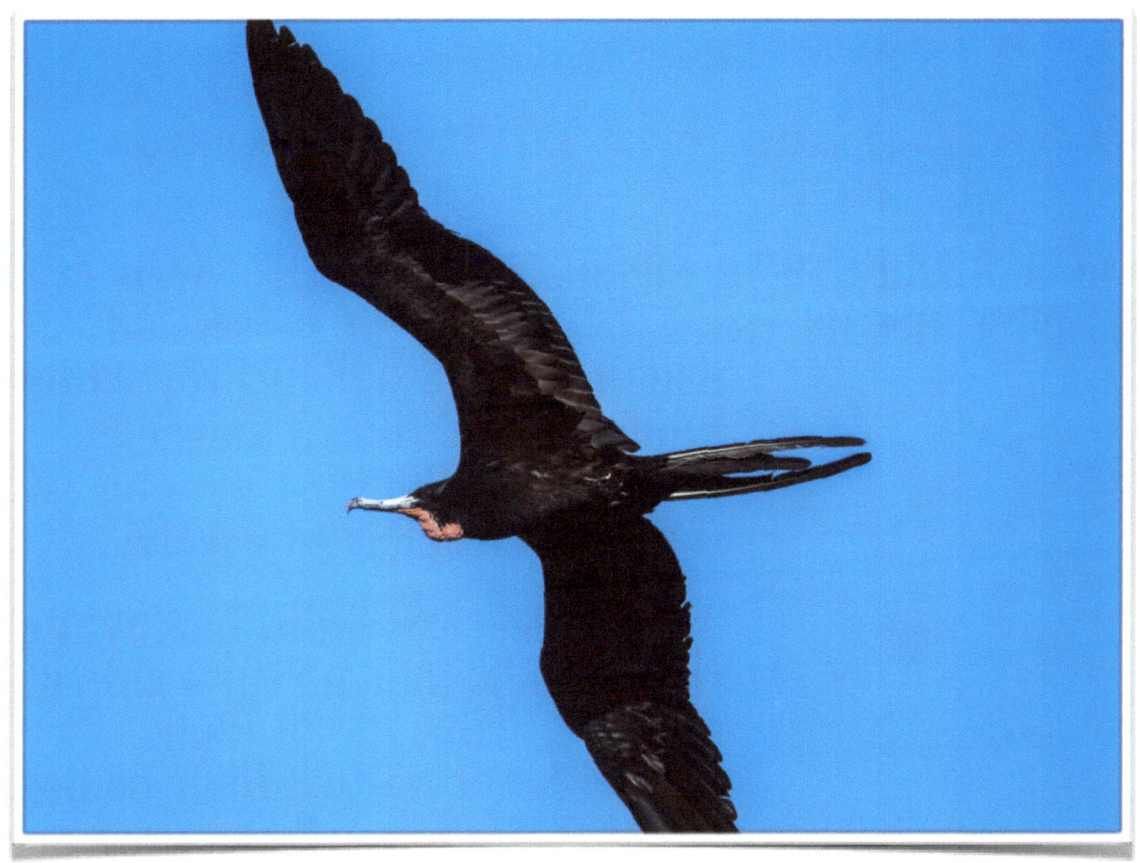

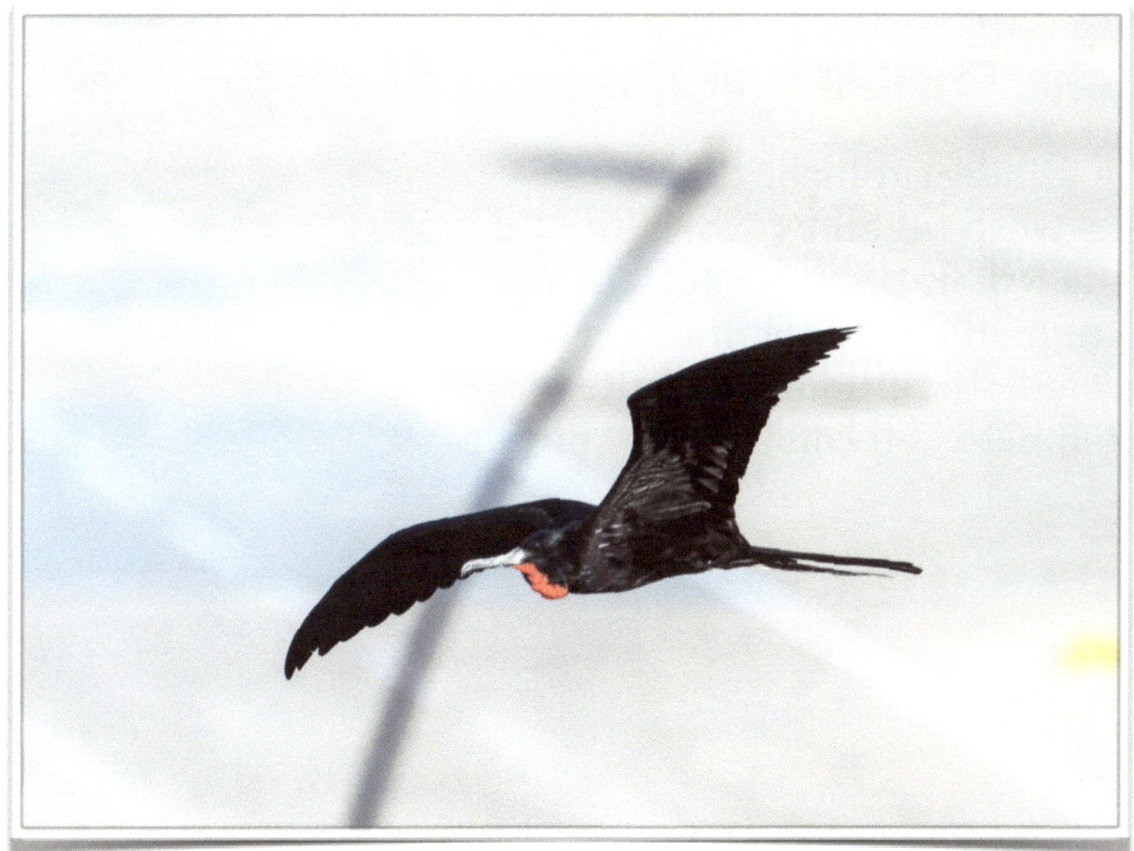

The Masked and Brown Boobies

The Masked and Brown Boobies are seabirds rarely seen inland. They dive for flying fish out in the ocean and usually swallow their prey while underwater. When a masked booby dives into the ocean for fish, it forms a torpedo-like wake.

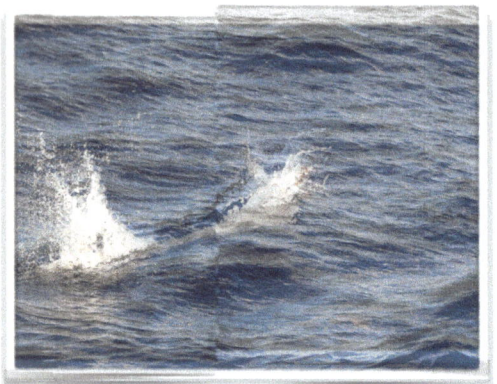

These birds can multi-task while flying along side a cruise ship at 25 knots. They preen their feathers and scratch their bodies.

They are very tenacious and can keep up with a cruise ship at high sea for hours hunting for fish.

All the photographs of these boobies were taken by Norman Wei with his Nikon D500 camera and 500 mm prime lens from the cruise ship Celebrity Silhouette in the high sea between Cuba and Espinola.

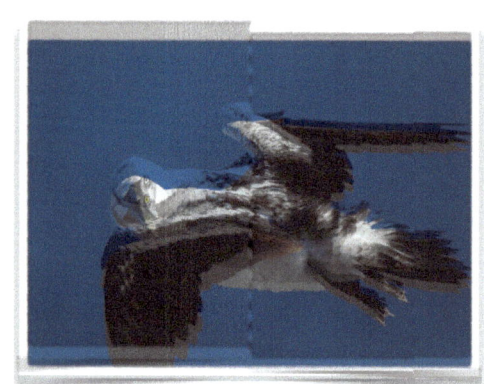

The Masked and Brown Boobies

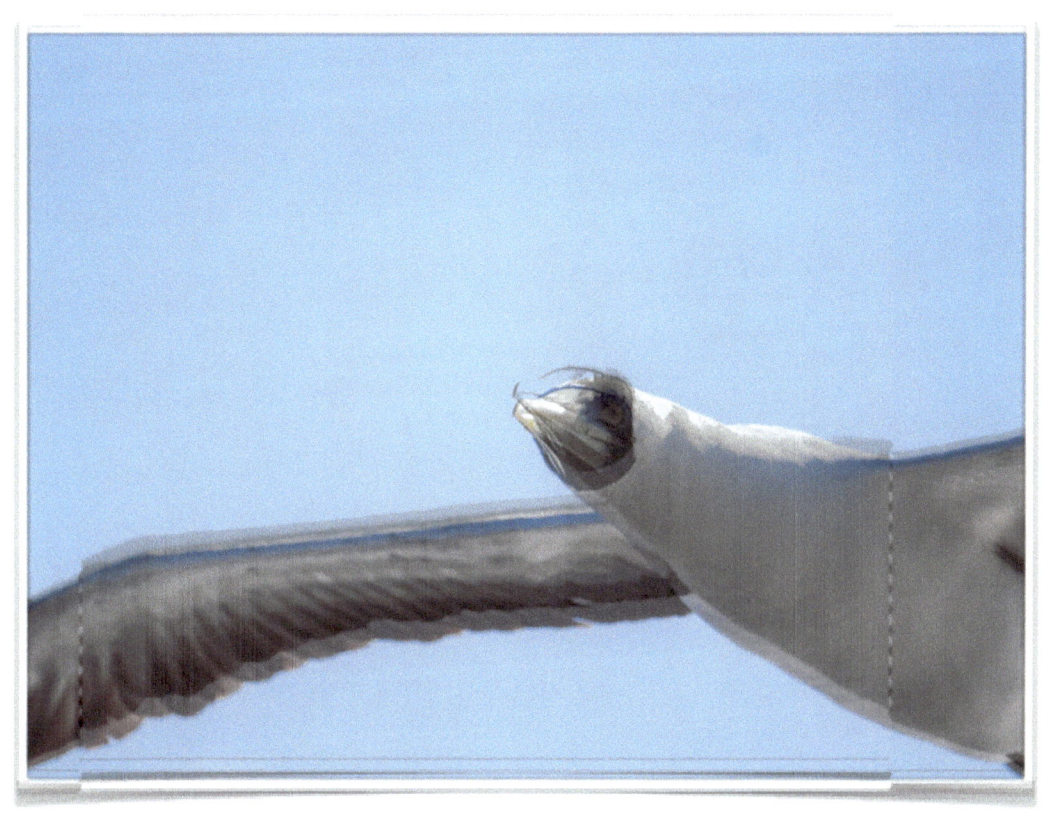

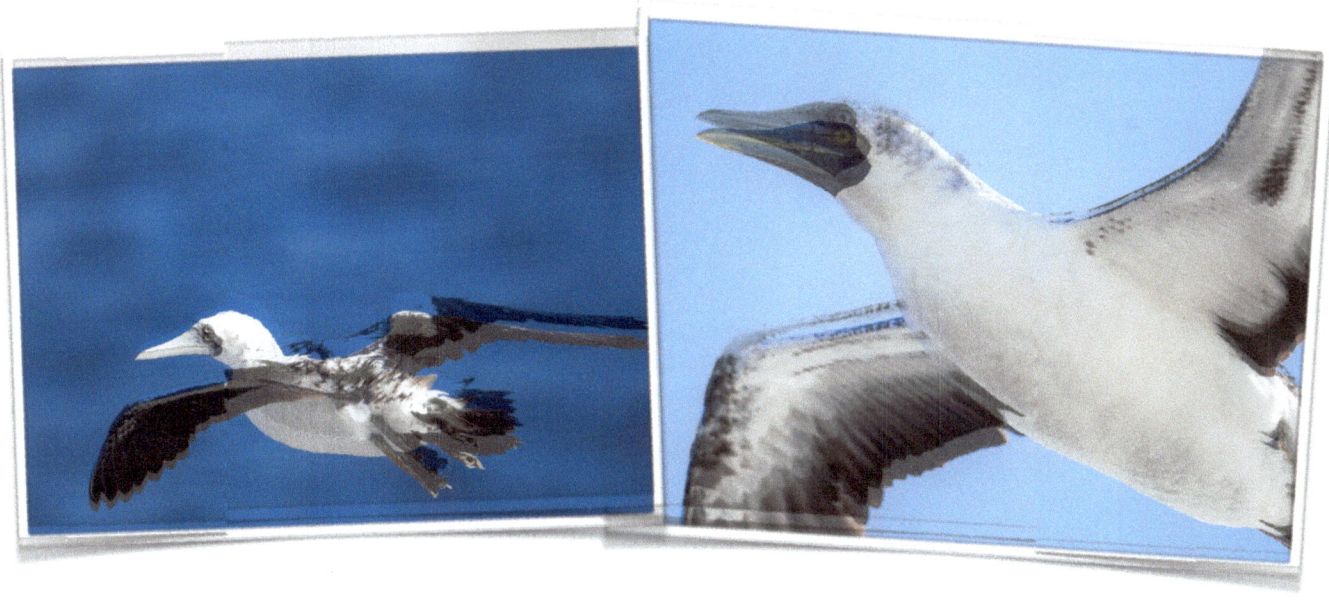

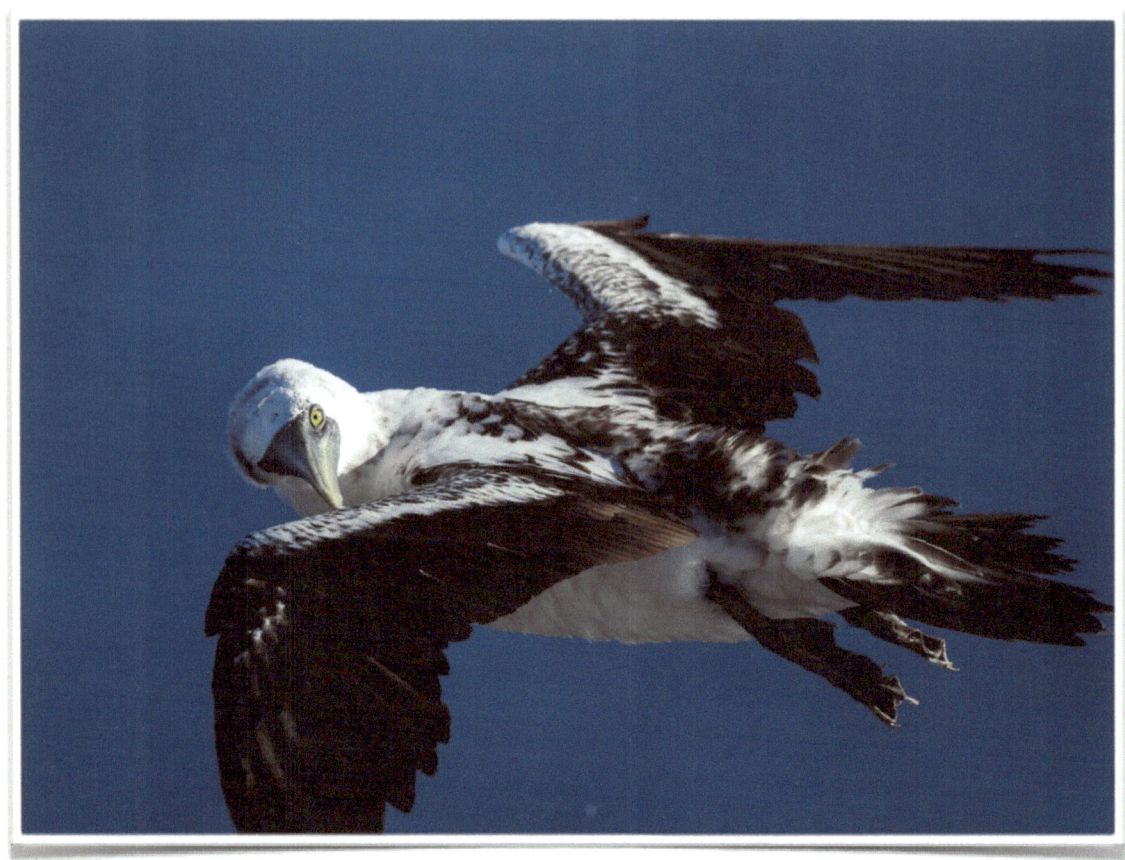

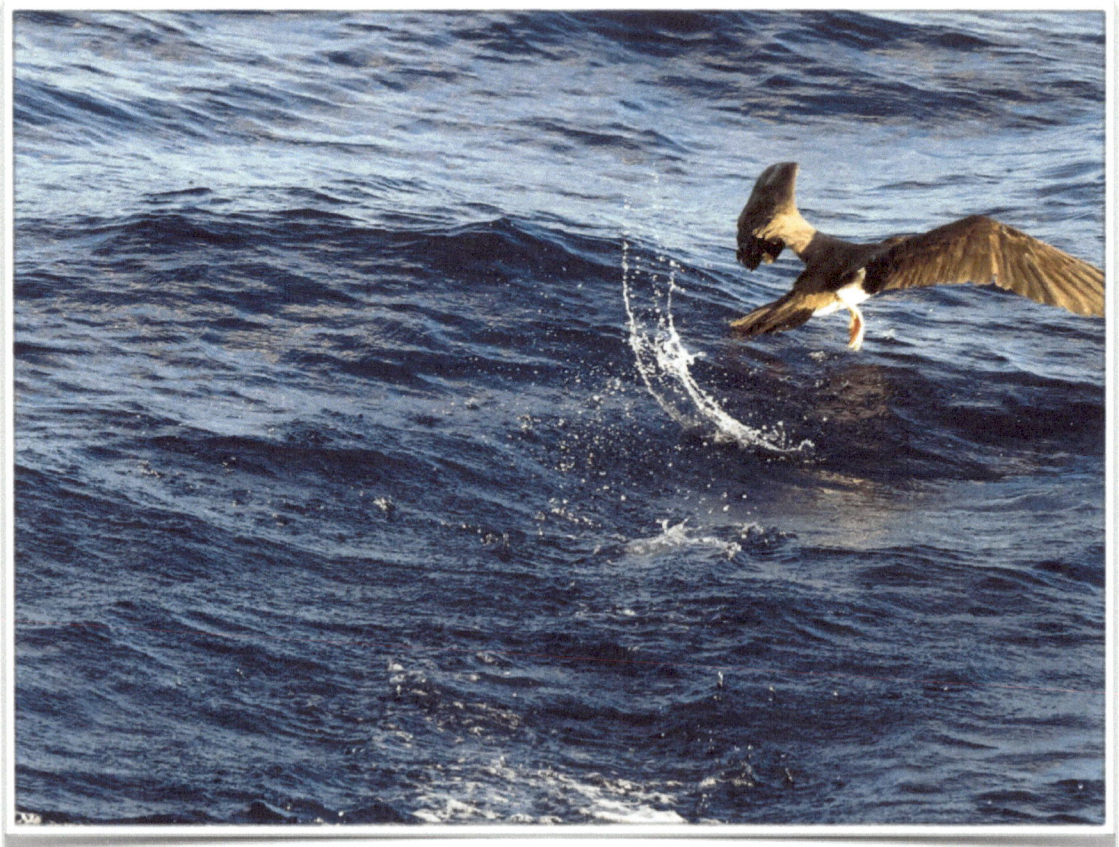

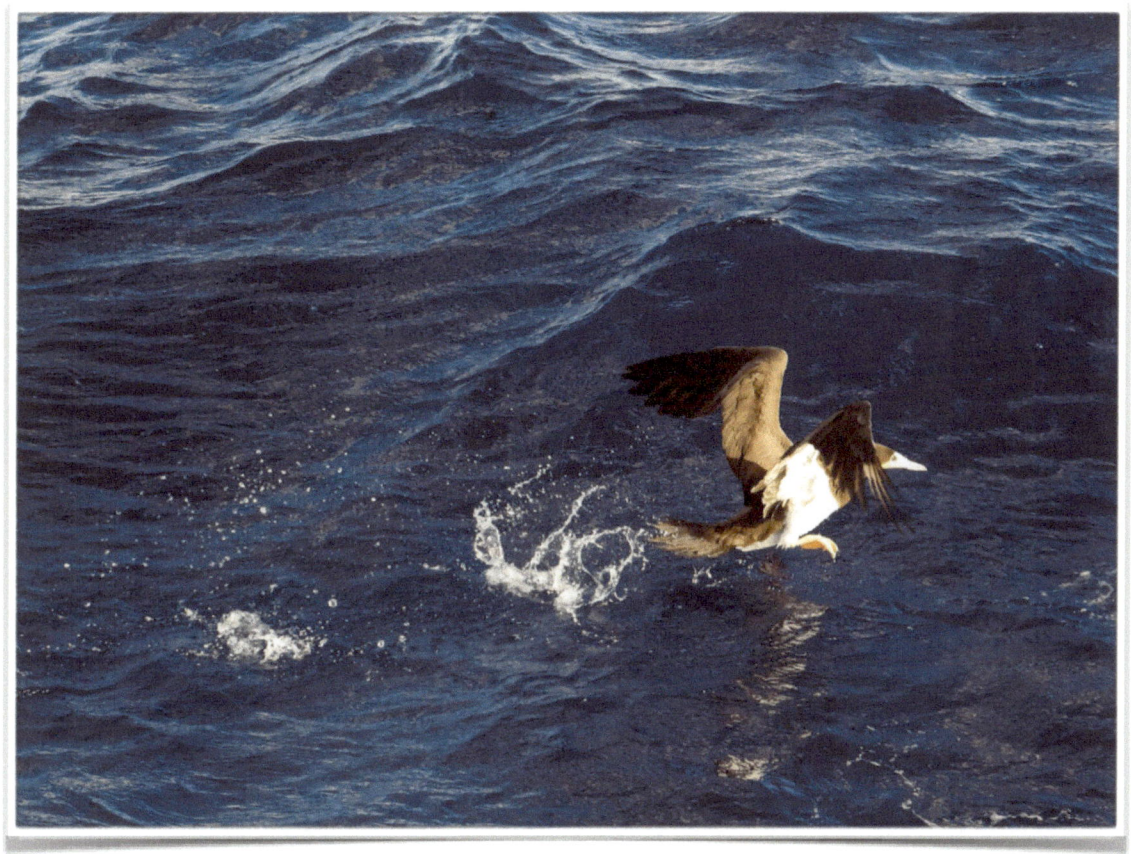
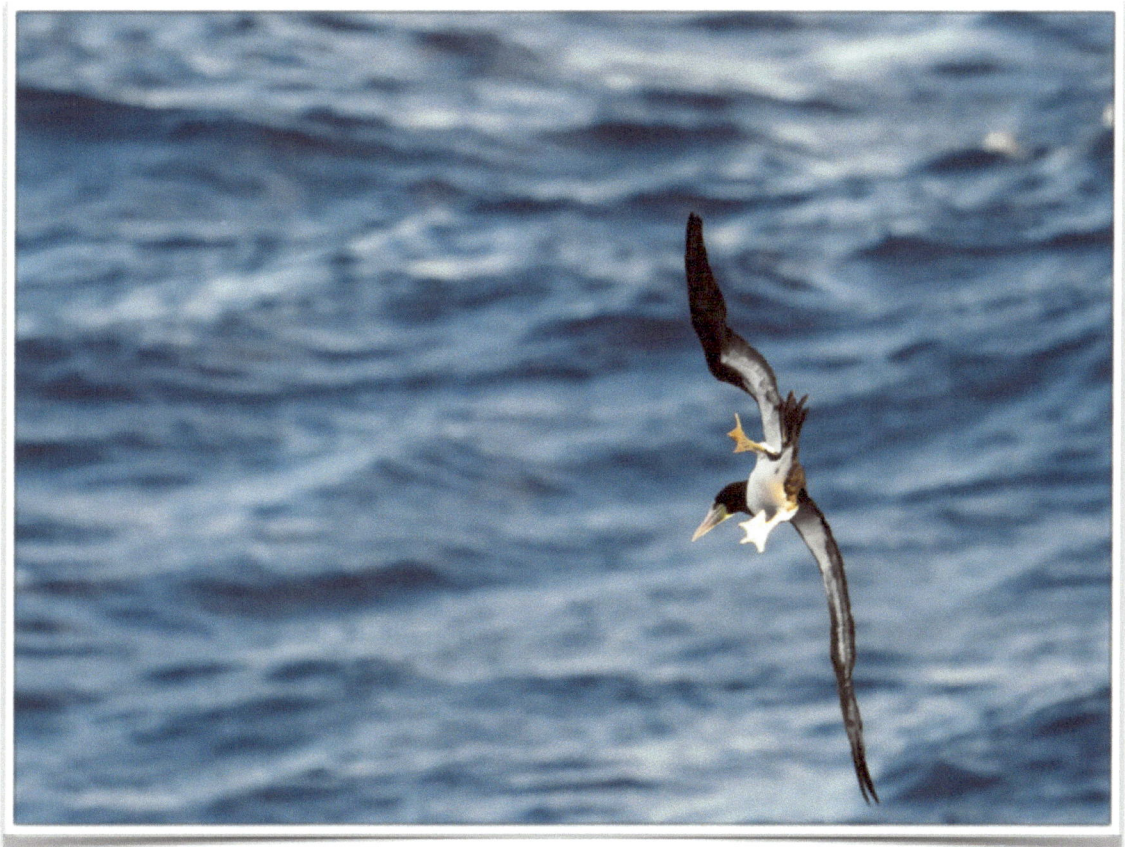

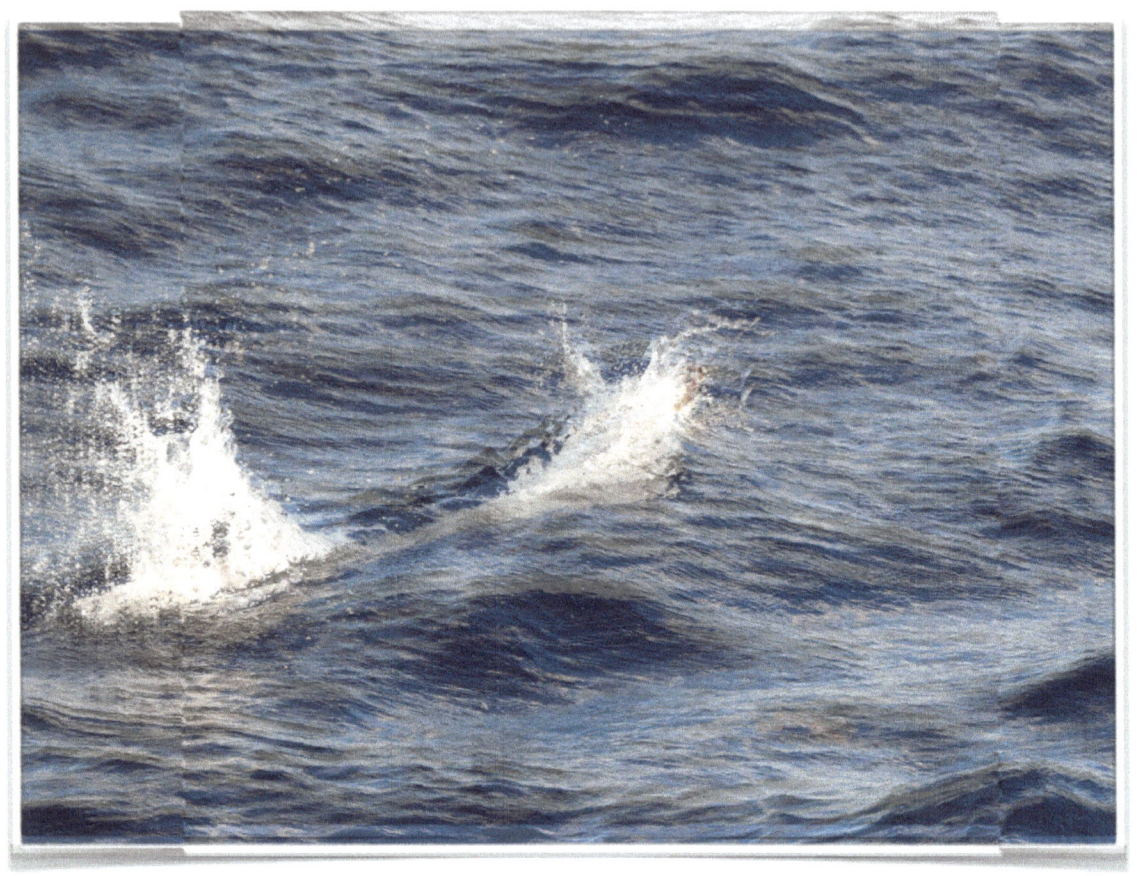
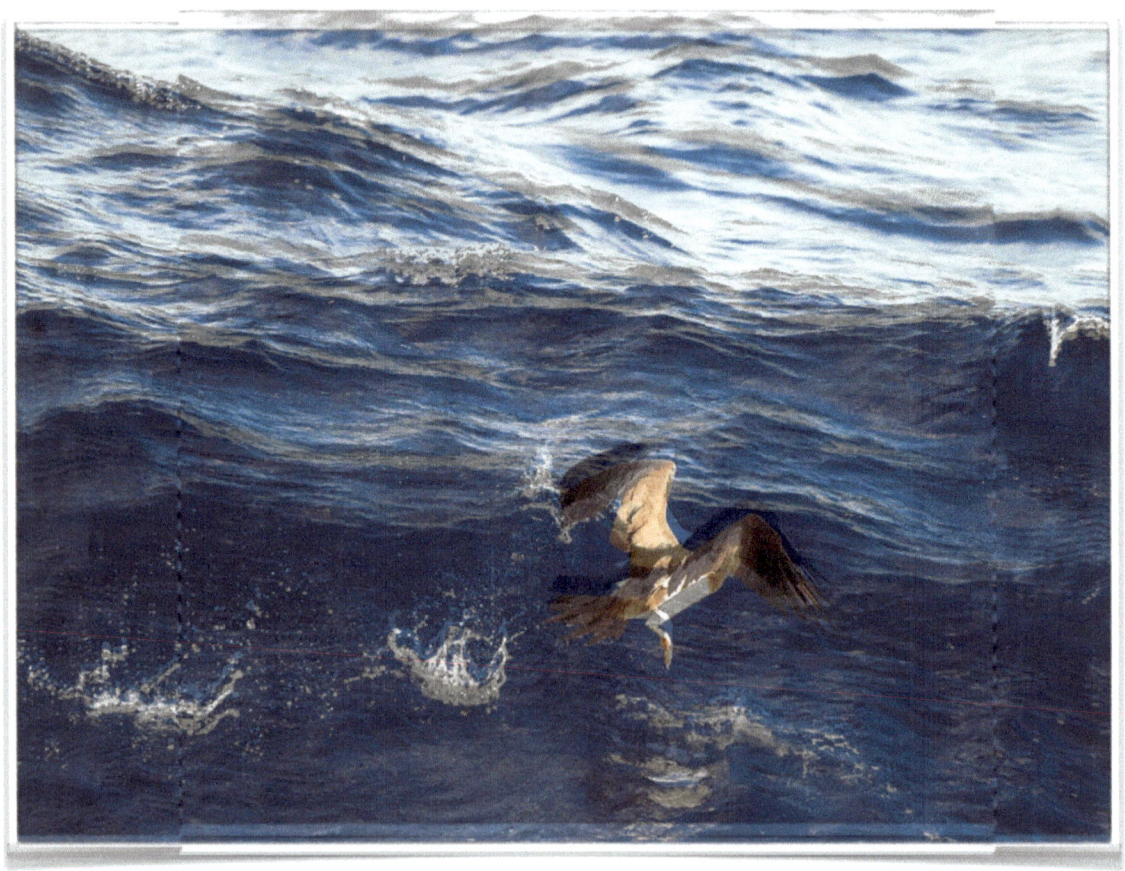

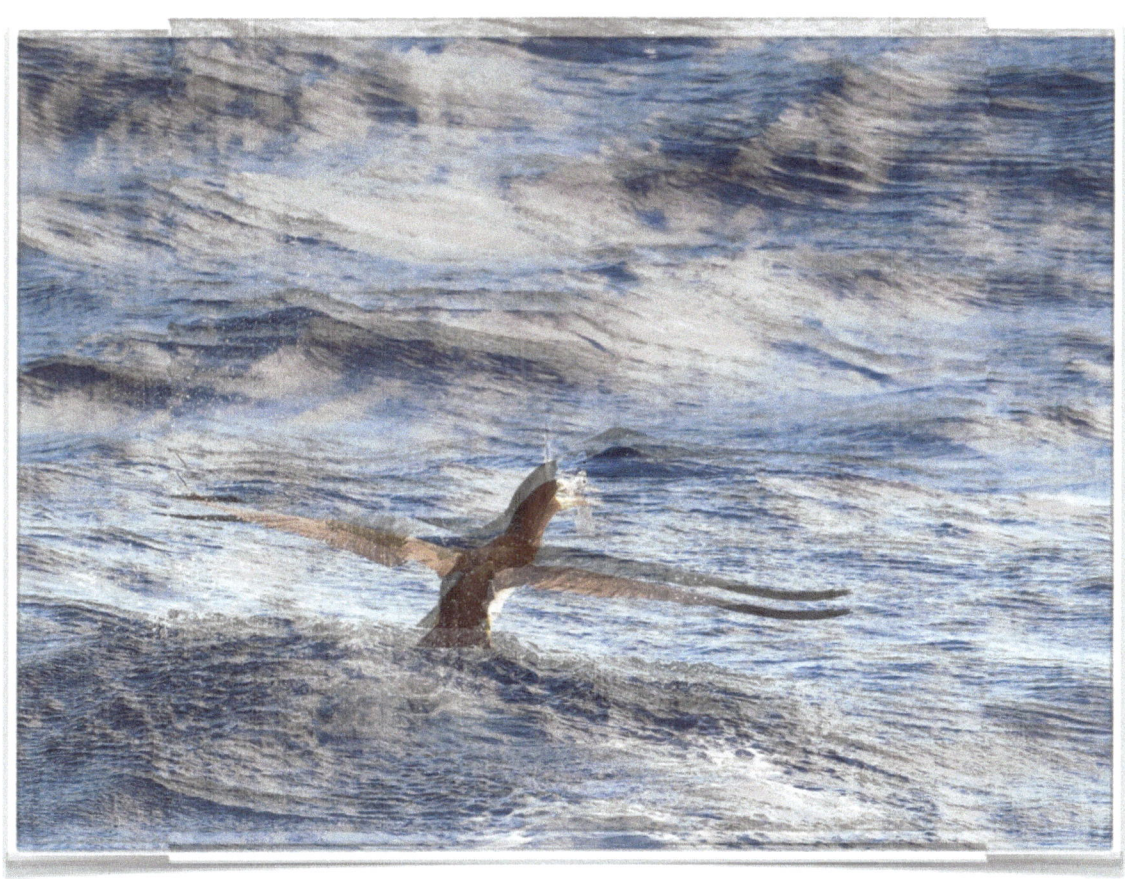

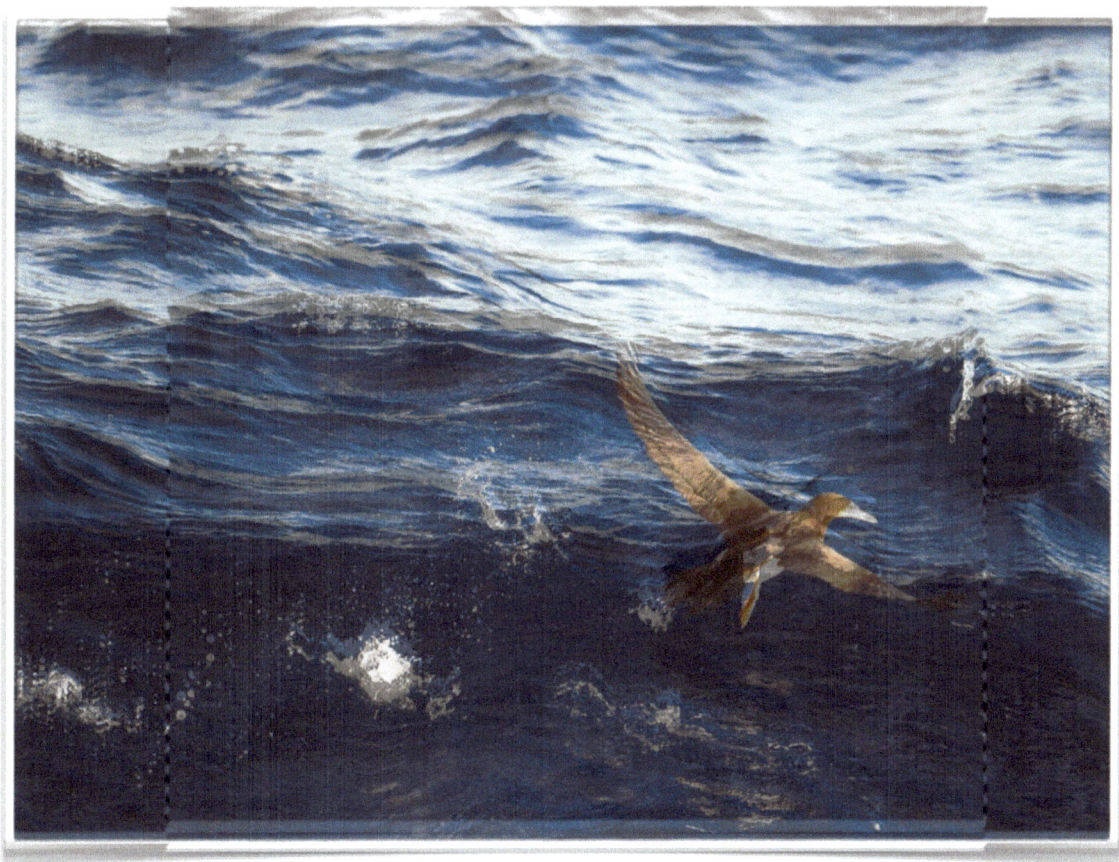

The American Flamingo

The American Flamingo has a very long "coat hanger" neck and long legs. Due to the presence of salt gland in 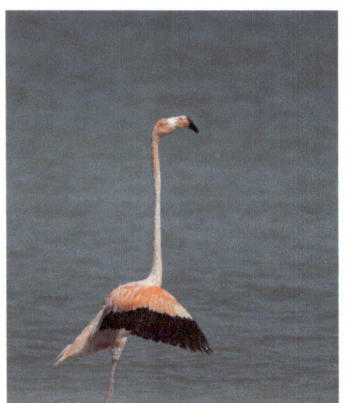 this bird, it is able to eat a very salty diet such as shrimps in very salty lagoons.

All the photographs of these flamingos were taken by Norman Wei with his Nikon D500 camera and 500 mm prime lens in Bonaire.

The American Flamingo

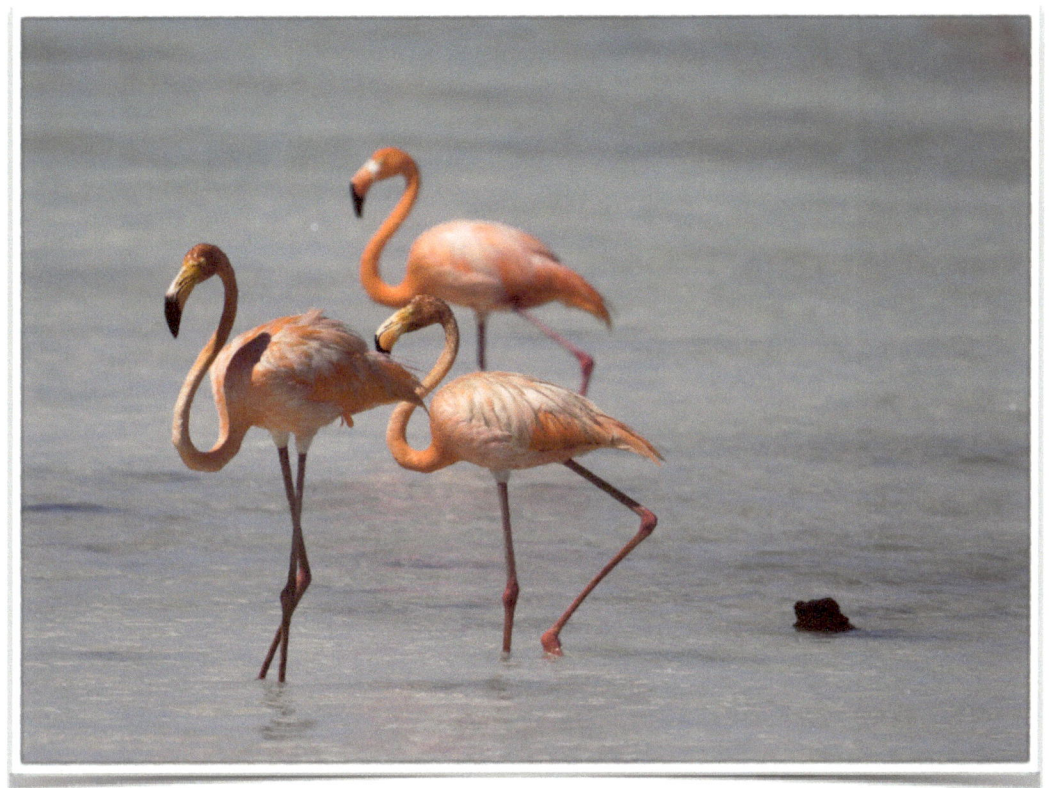

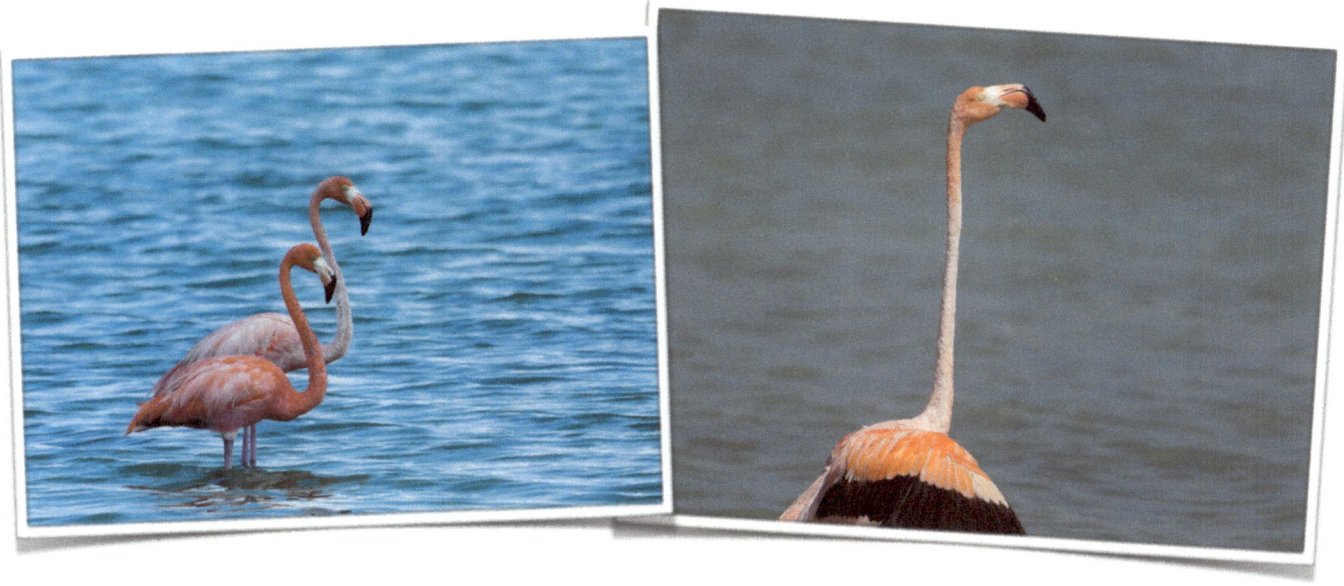

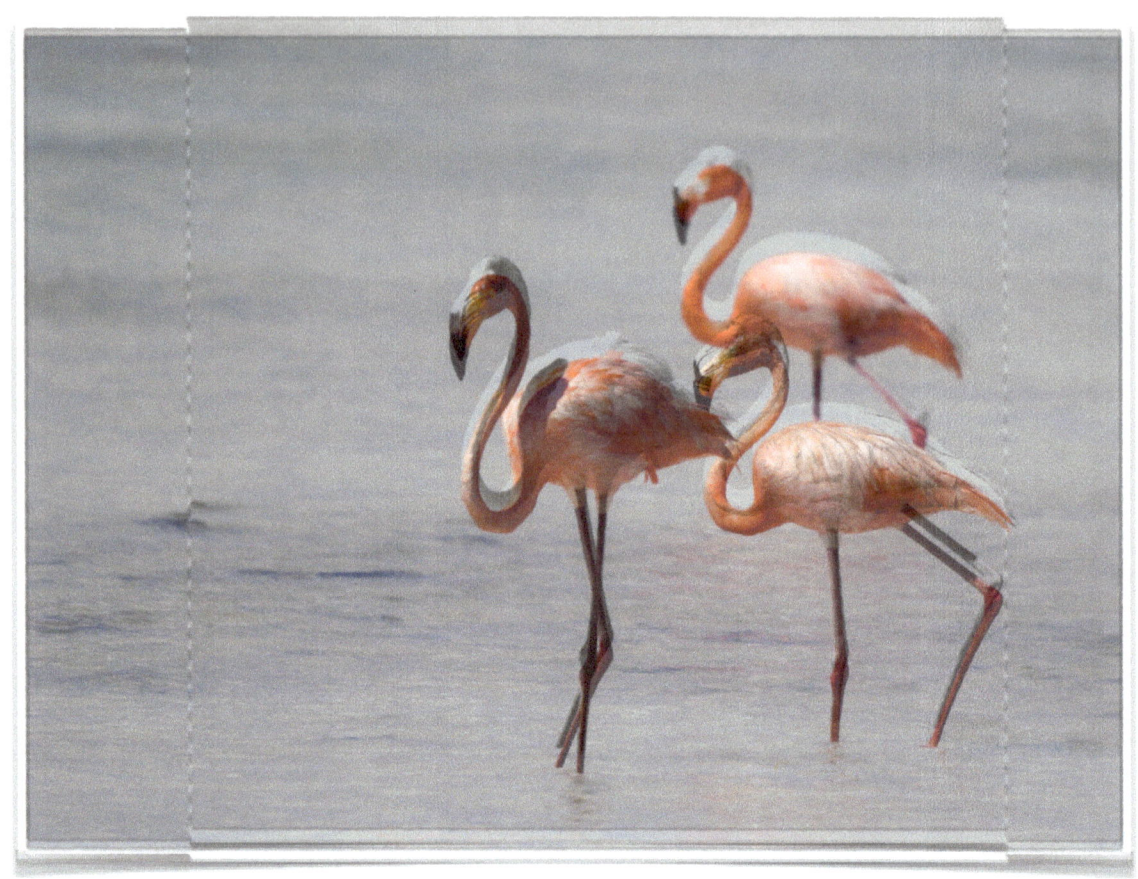
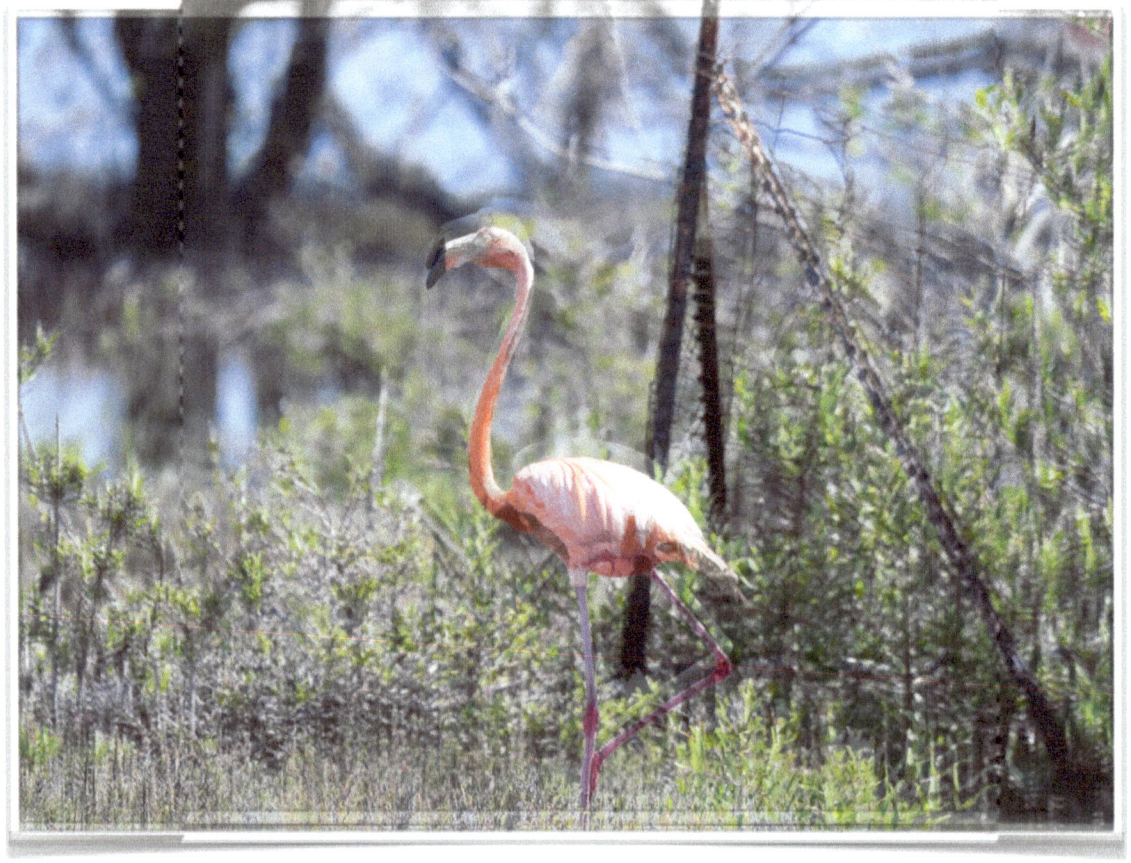

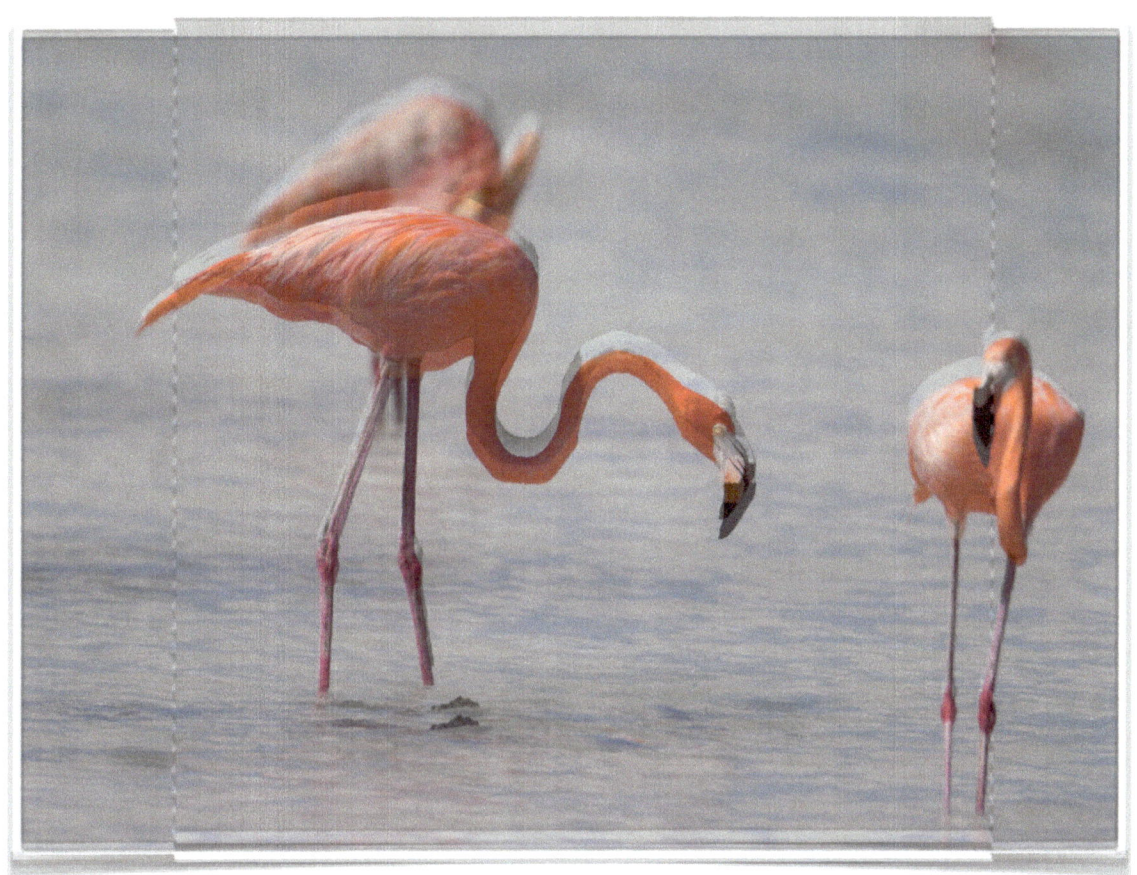

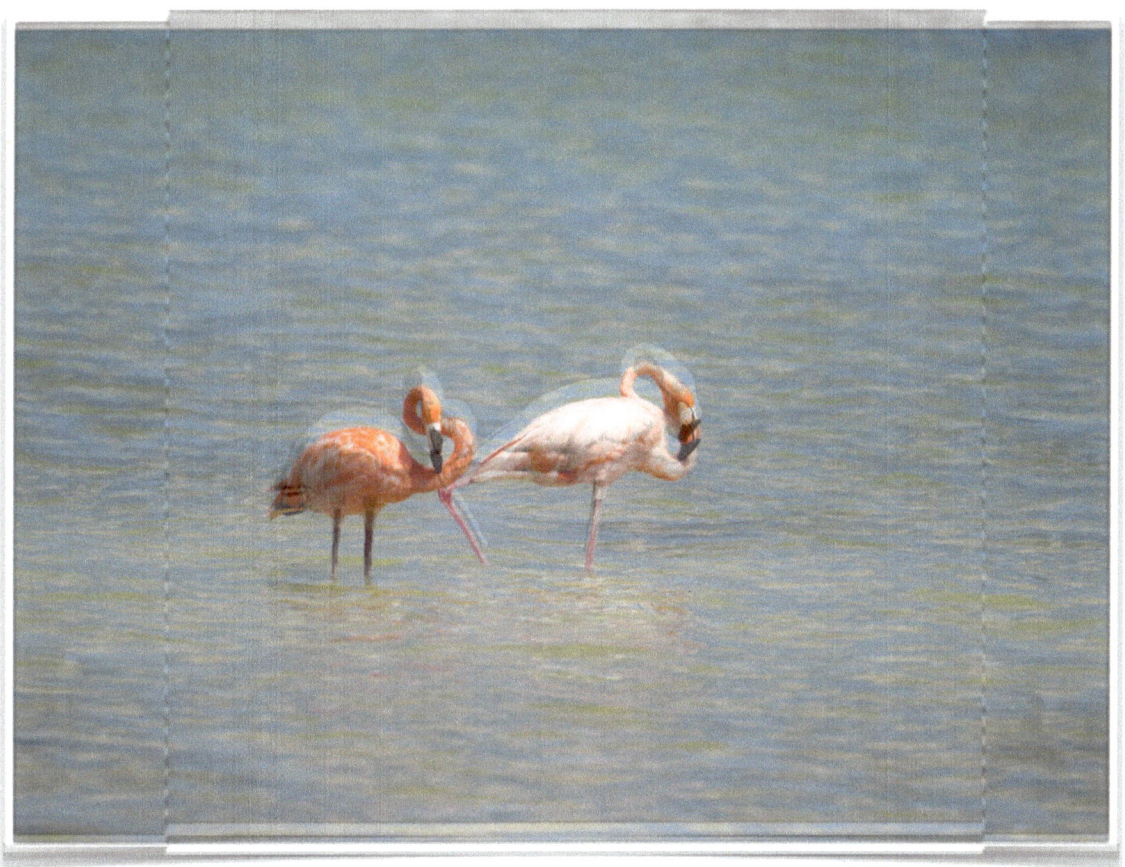

The Hummingbirds

Bonaire has two species of **hummingbirds**: The Ruby Topez and the blue-tailed emerald hummingbird. The green-breasted mango hummingbird is found in Cozumel, Mexico.

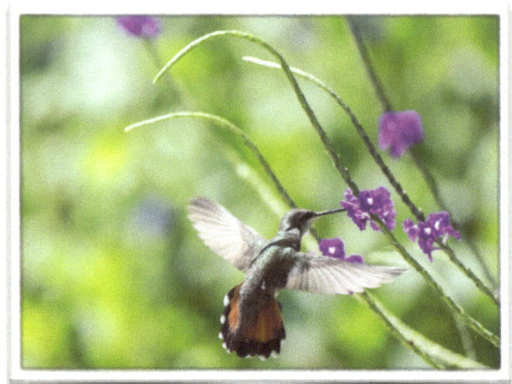

All the photographs were taken by Norman Wei with his Nikon D500 camera and 500 mm prime lens in Bonaire and Cozumel, Mexico.

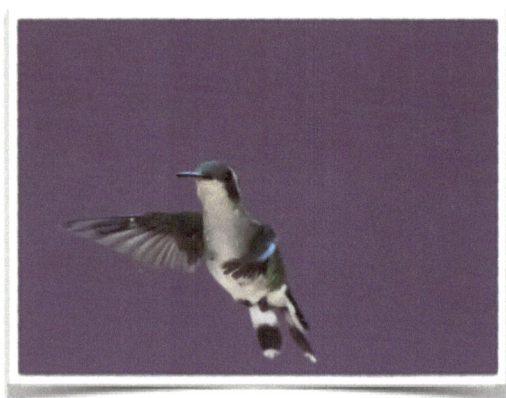

The Hummingbird

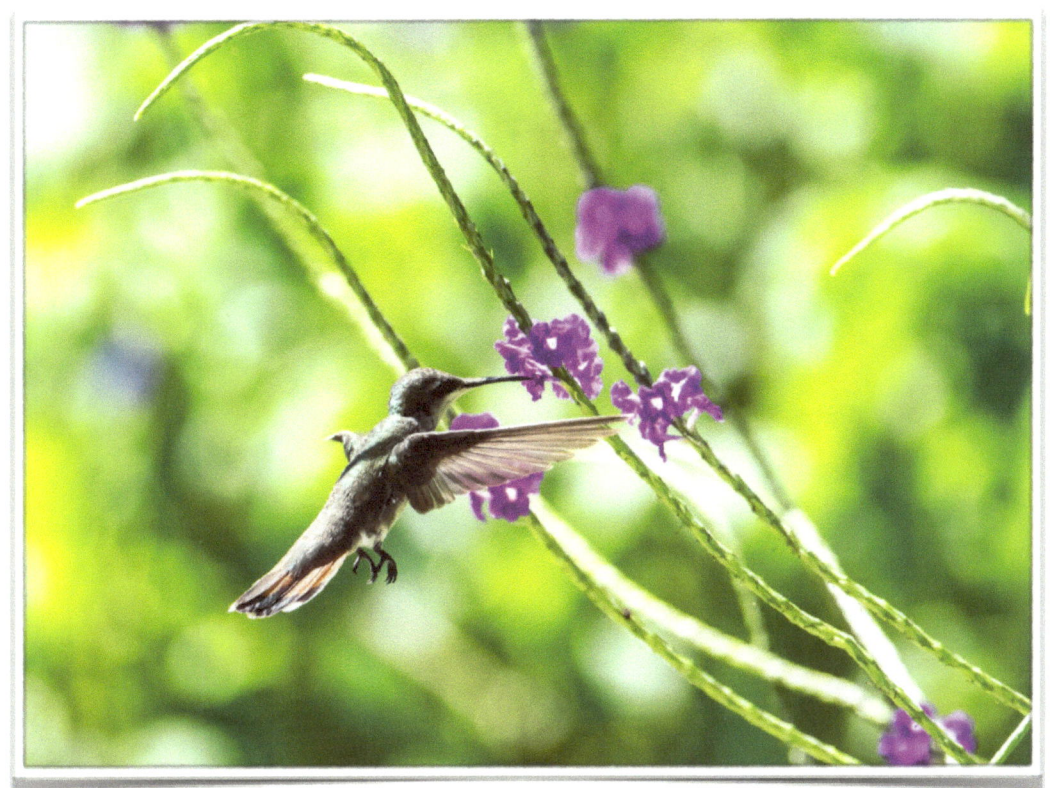

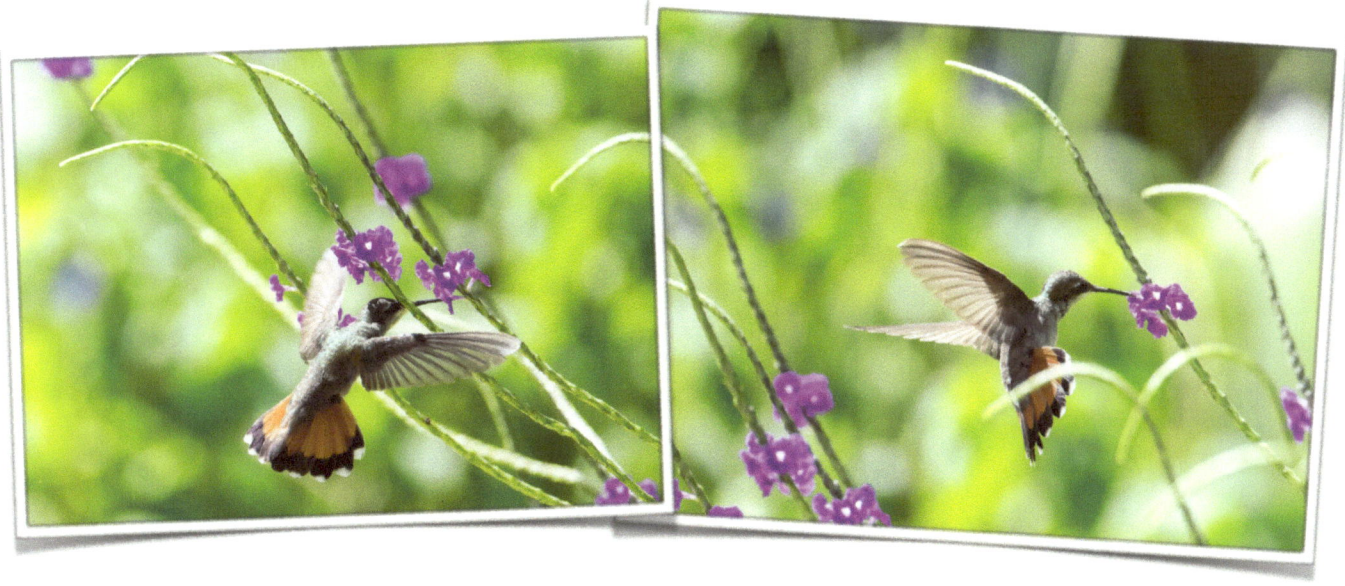

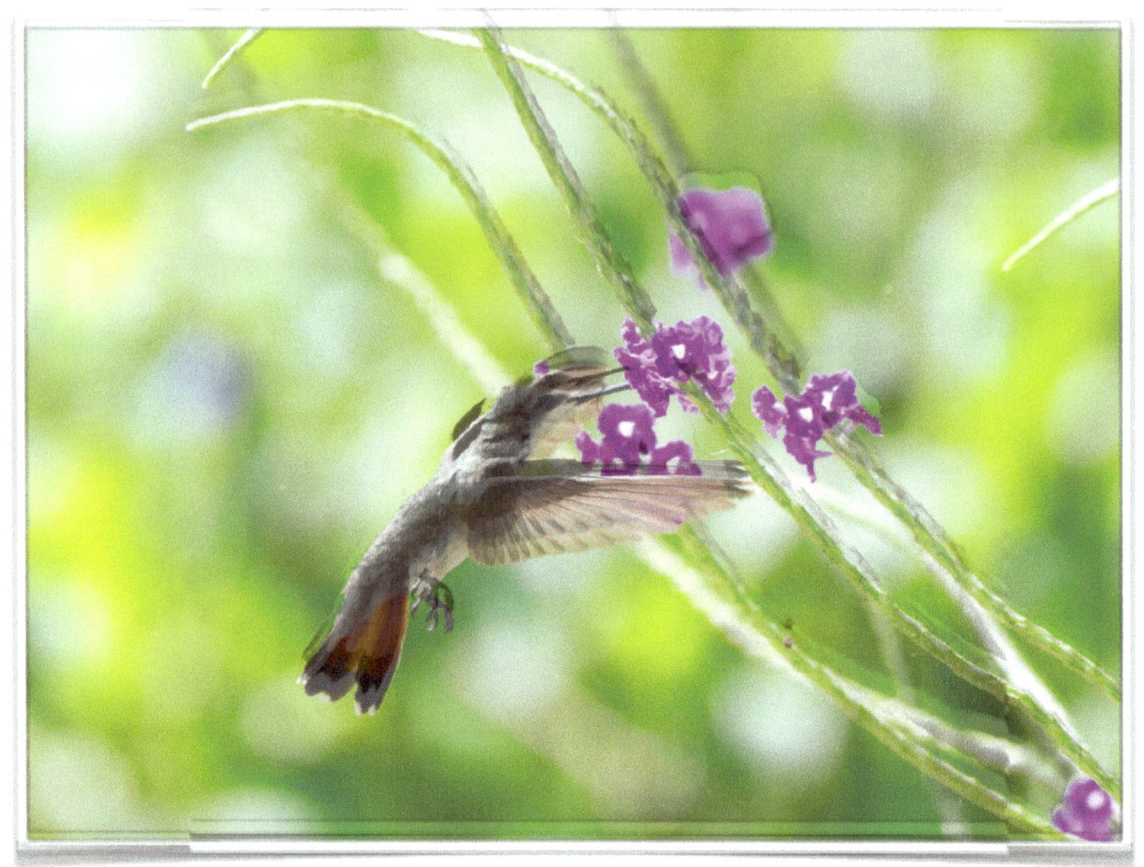

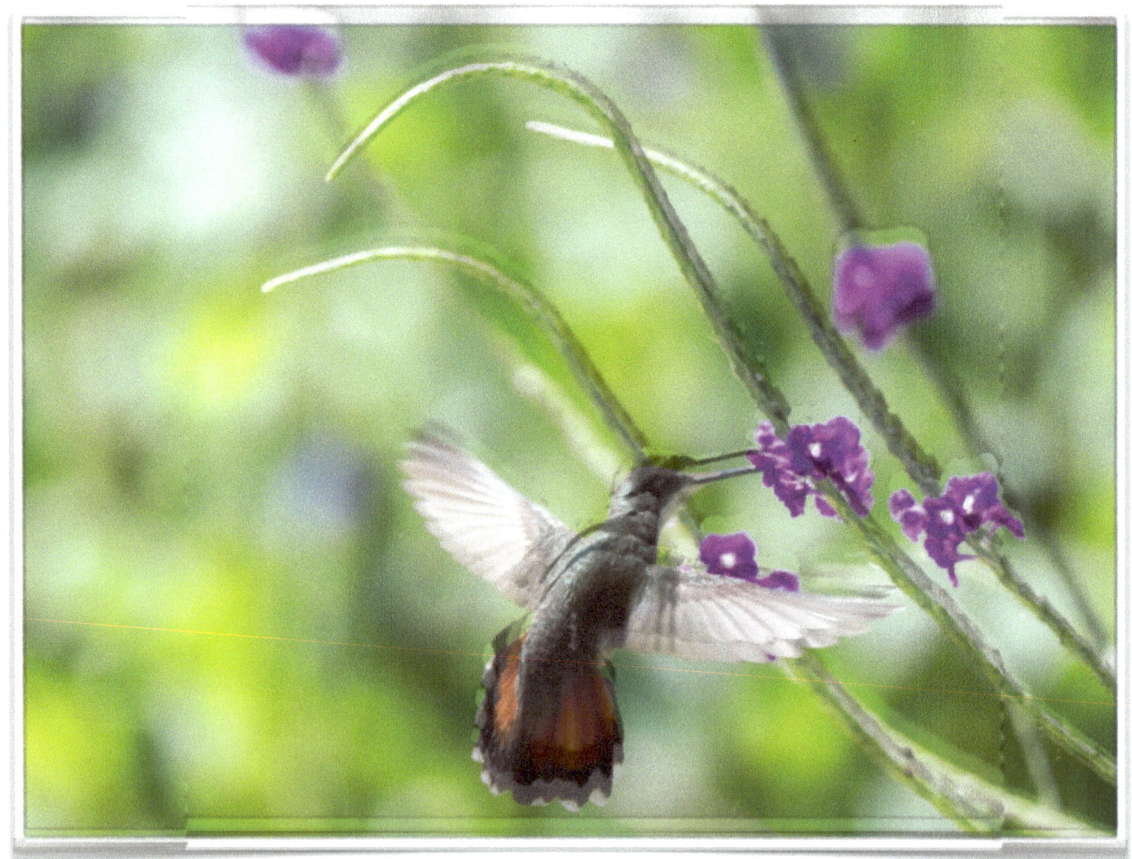

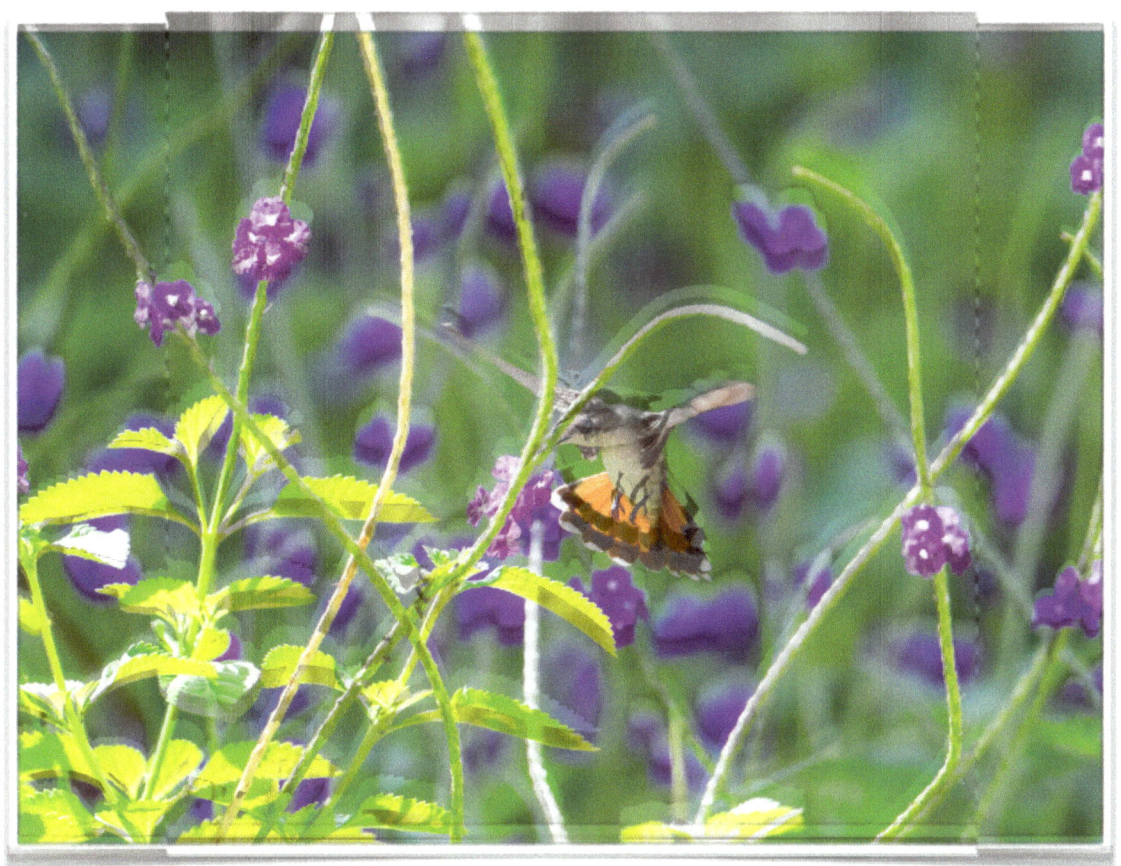
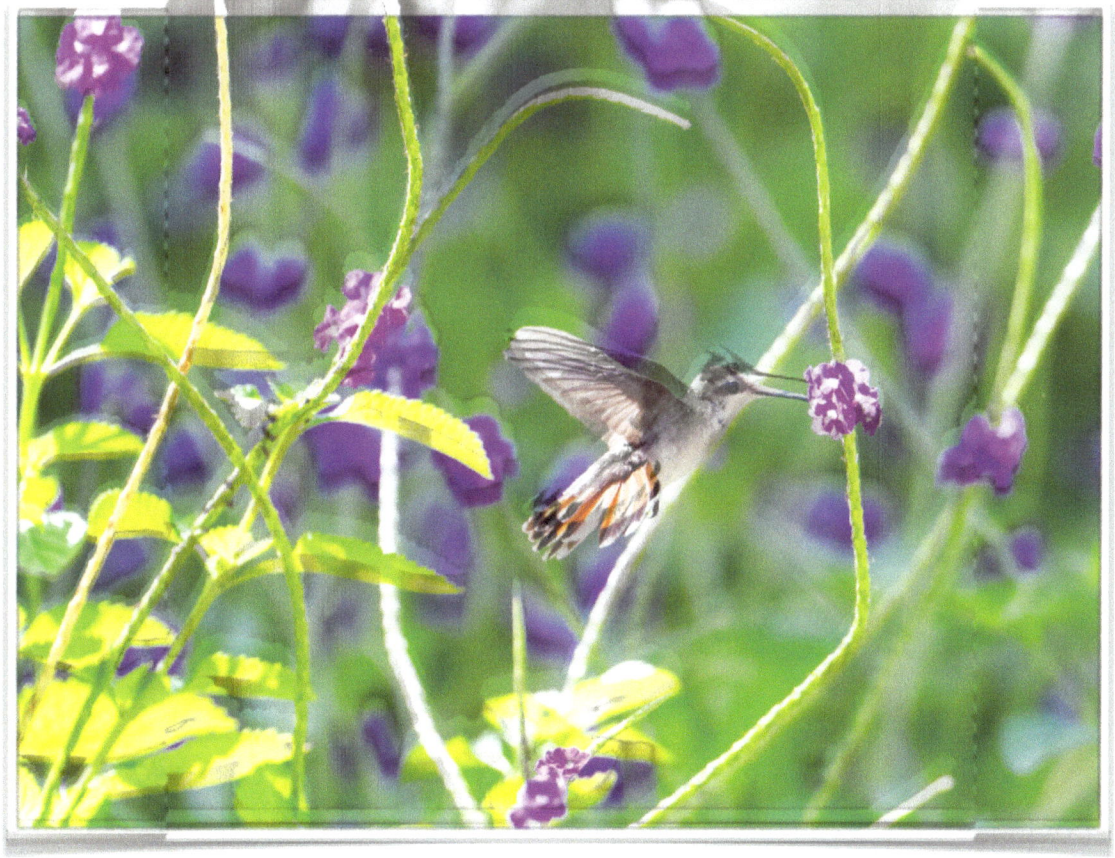

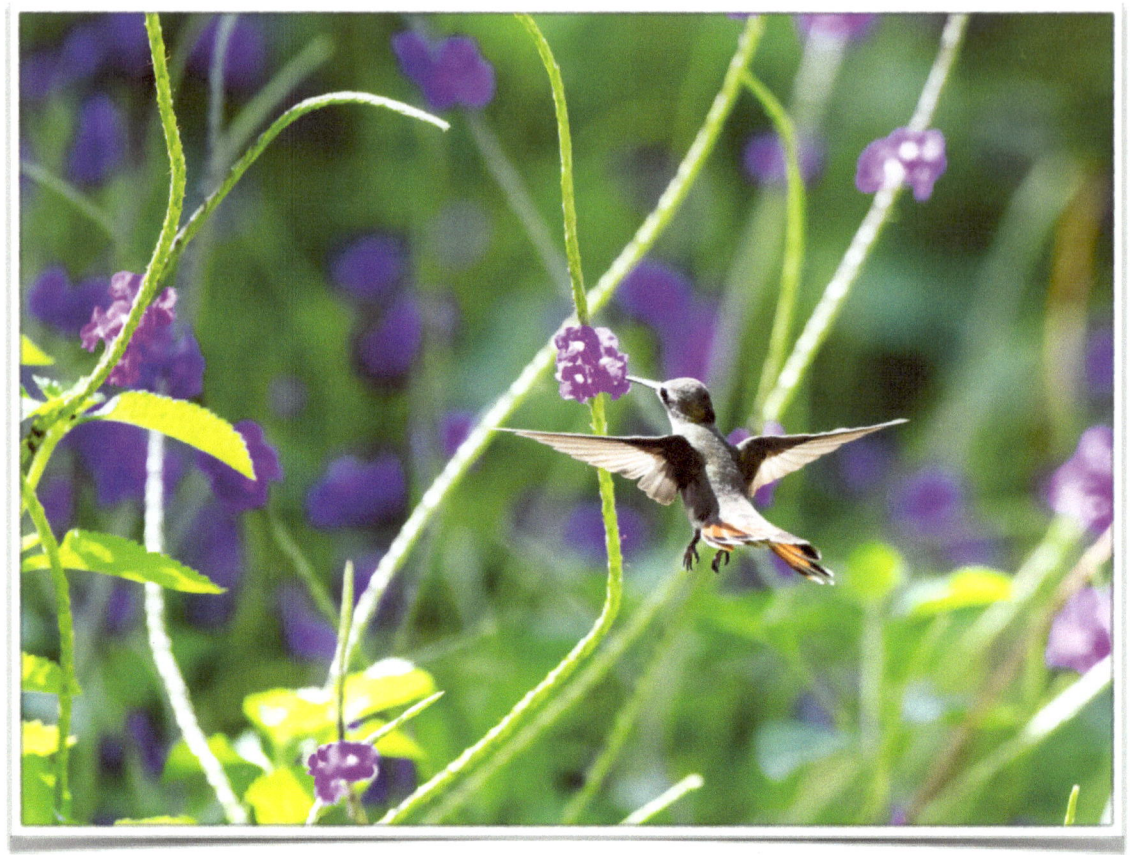
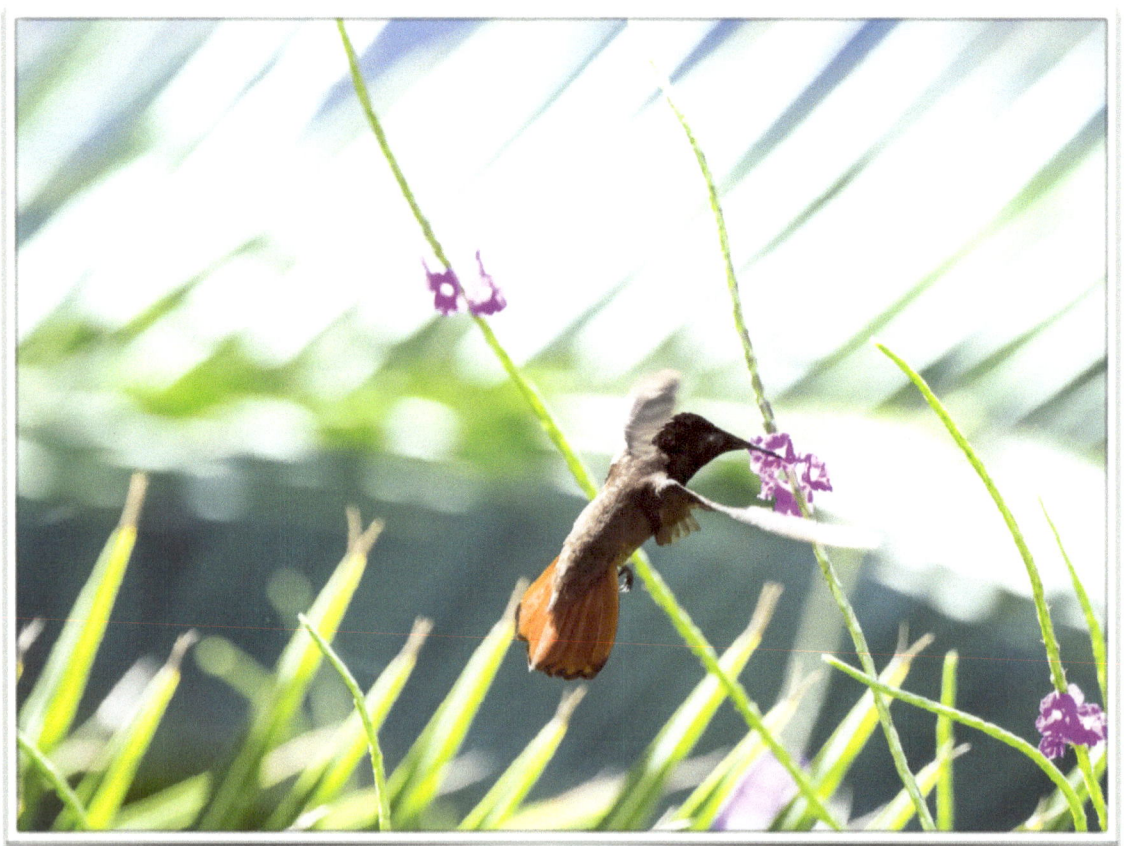

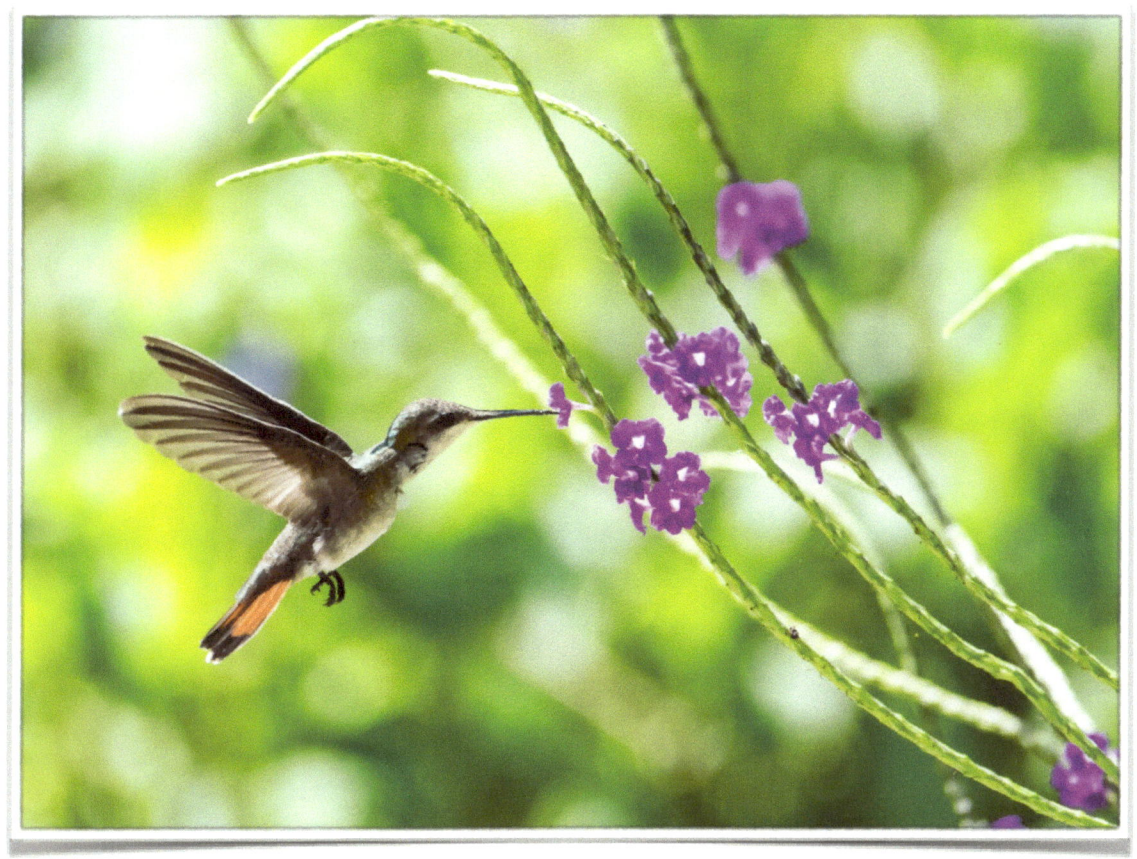

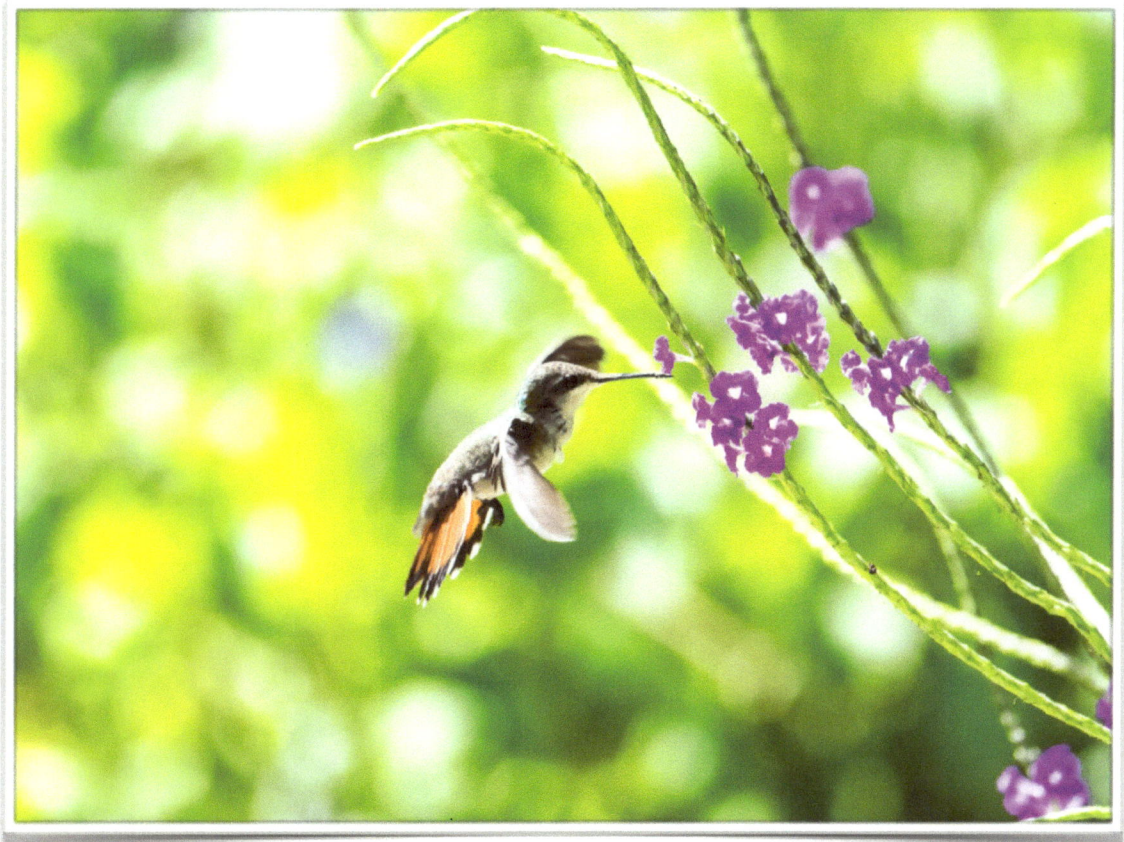

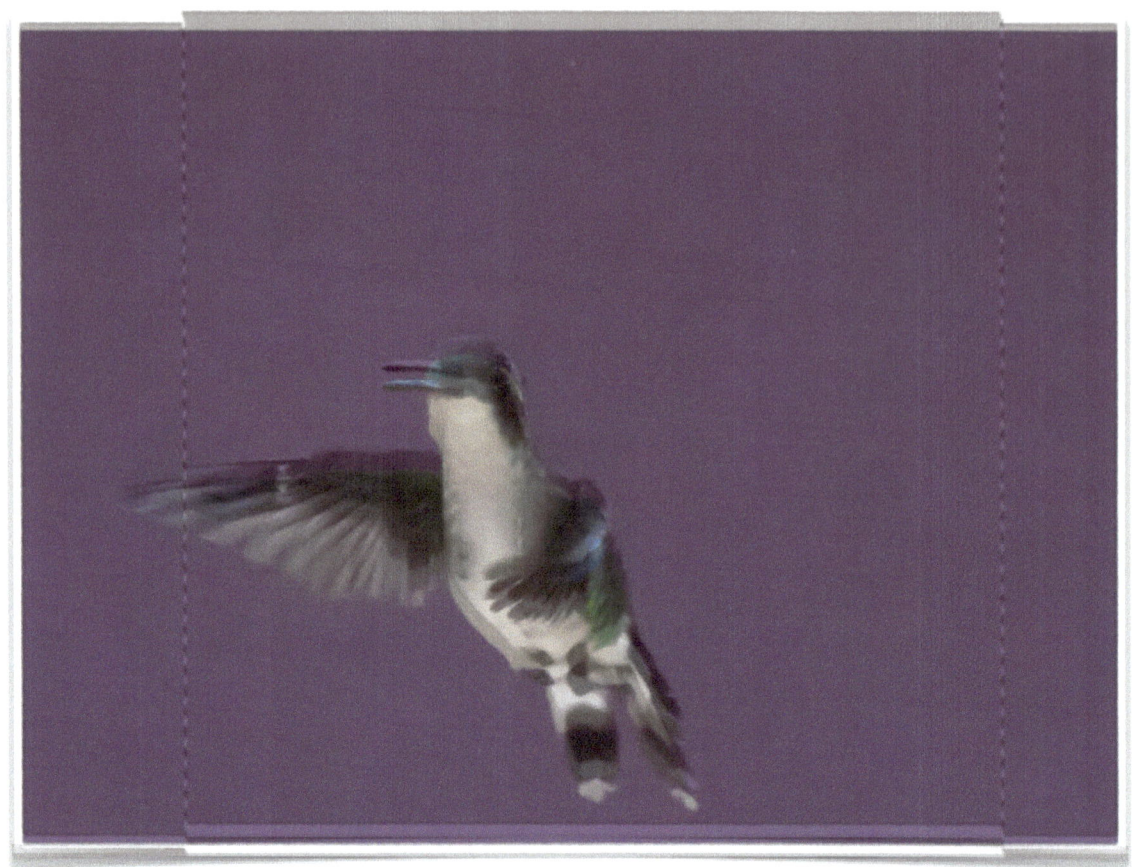
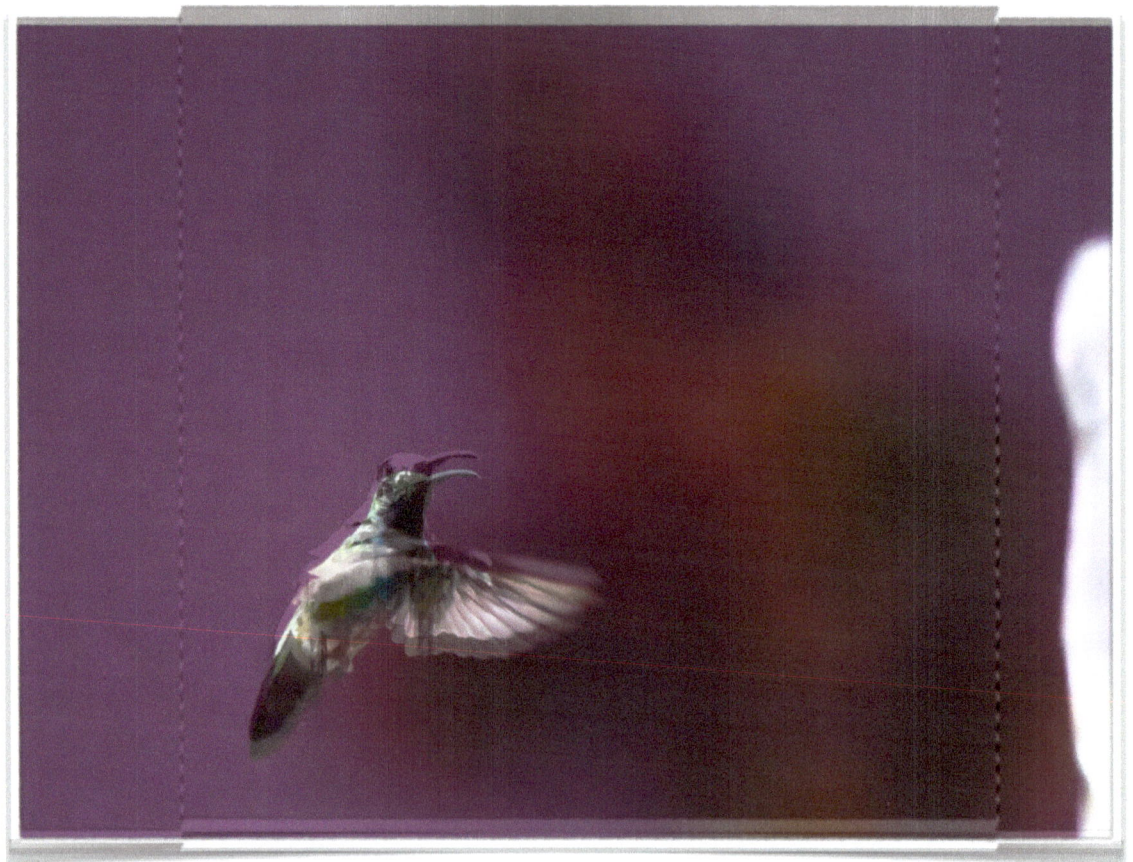

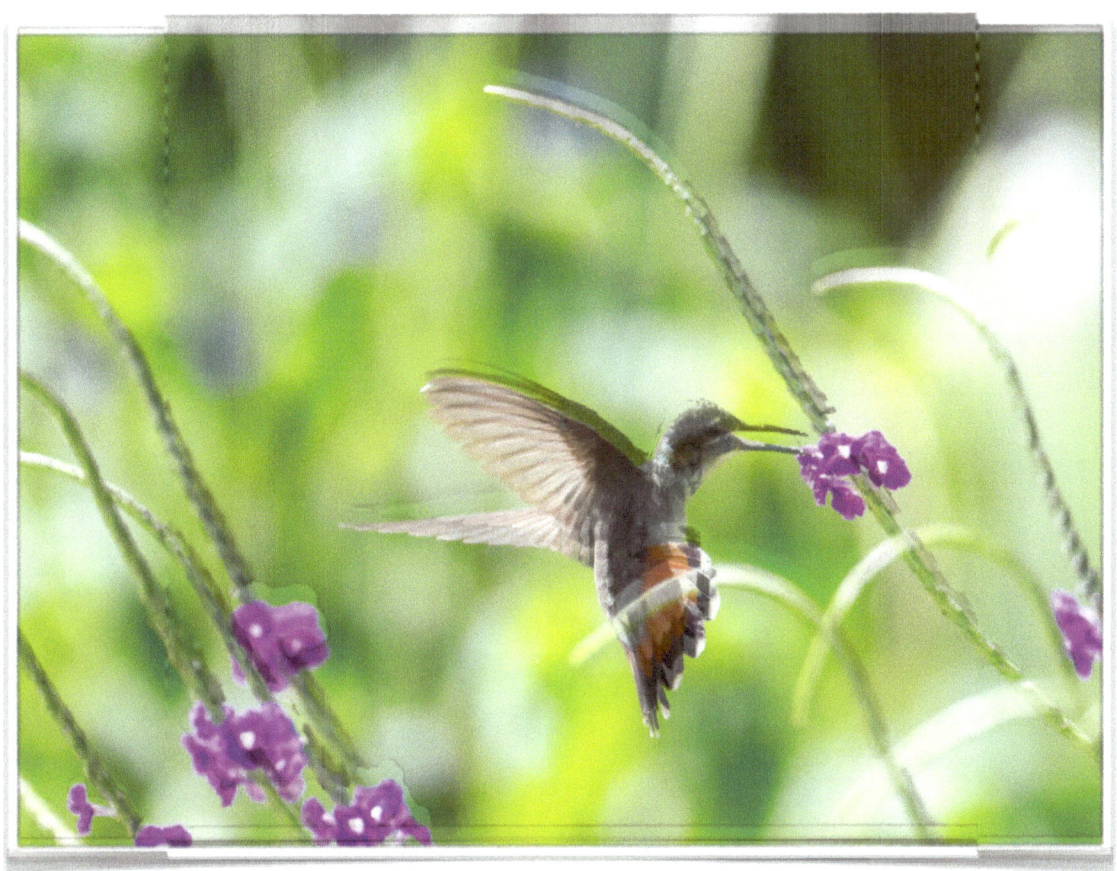

The Crested Caracara

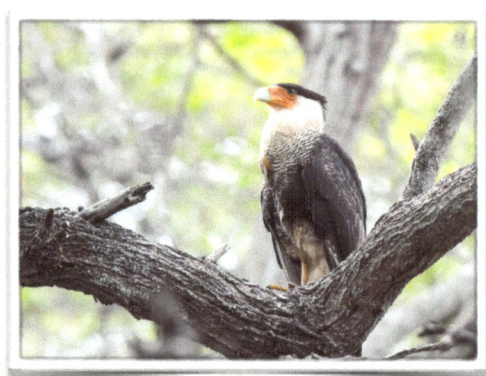

The Crested Caracara is a bird of prey found in Bonaire and Mexico. It is basically a flat-headed falcon with long legs and a dark cap on its head that looks like a bad hair piece. It behaves like a vulture and is sometimes referred to as the "Mexican buzzard".

There is a long history of this bird. Fossil remains of this bird has been found in California's La Brea Tar Pit and also in Mexico.

The Crested Caracara is a bird of open habitats such as grassland, pastures or cacti. They feed on roadkills and other preys and they often hang out with vultures.

All the photographs of the Crested Caracara in this book were taken by Norman Wei with his Nikon D500 camera and 500 mm prime lens in the Washington National Park in Bonaire.

The Crested Caracara

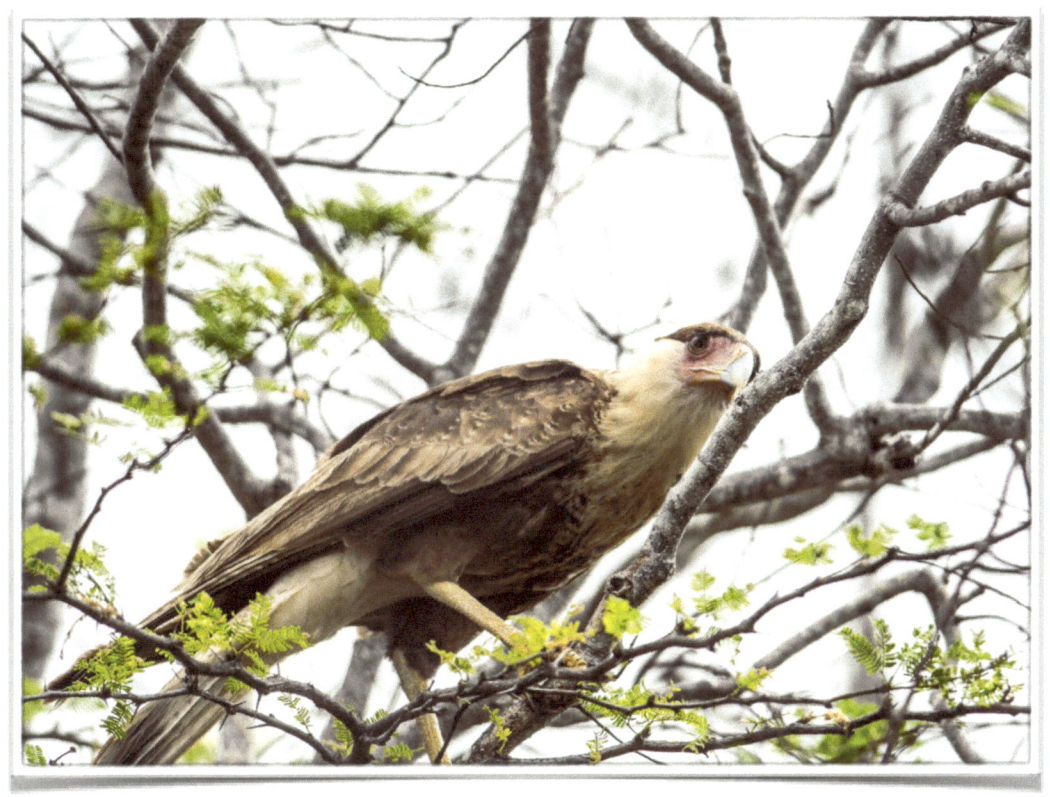

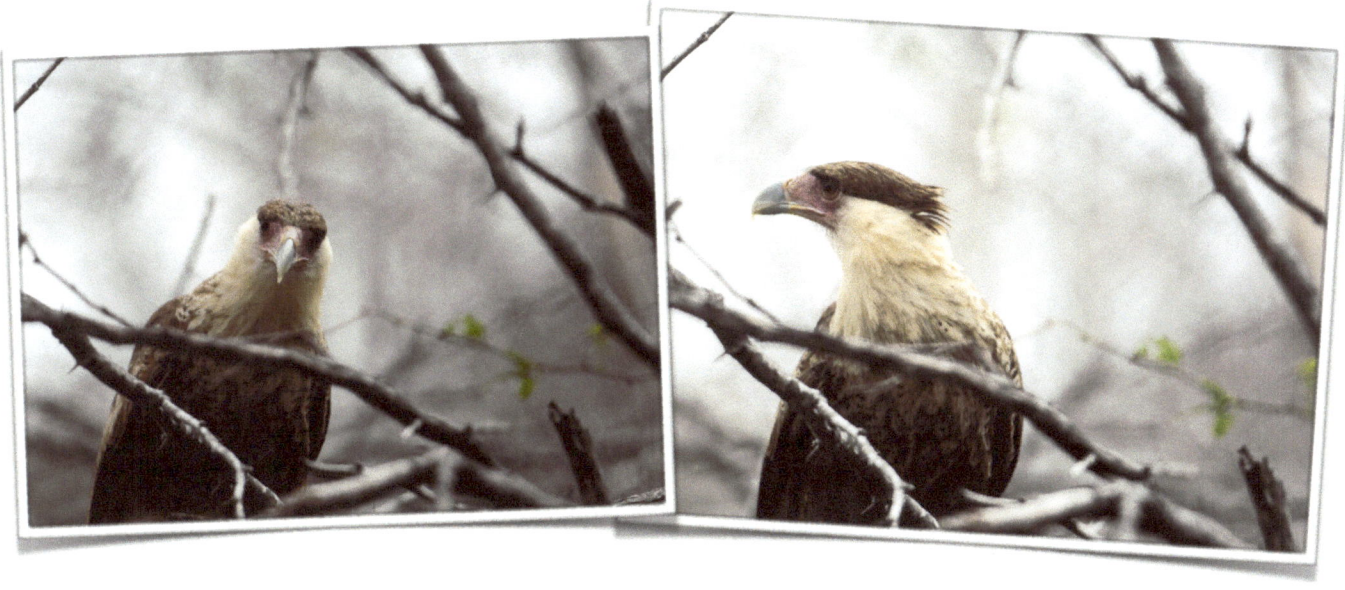

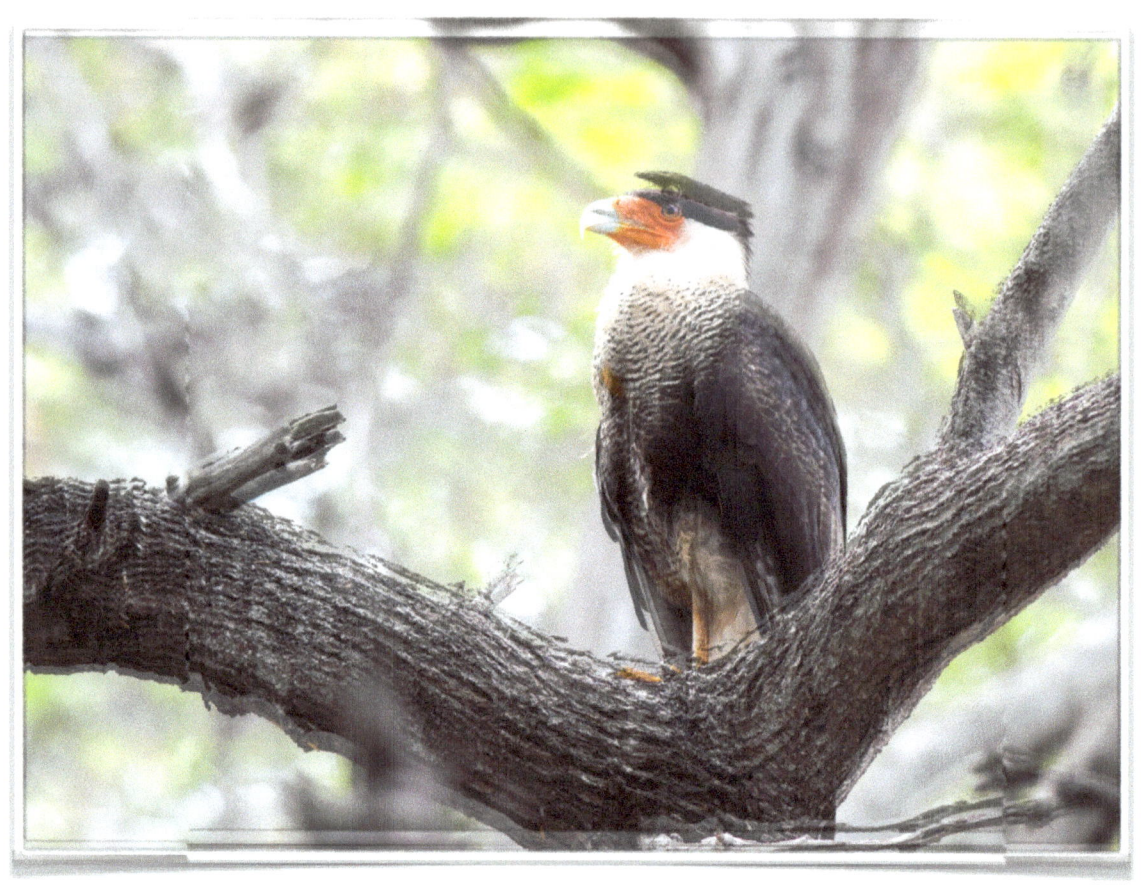
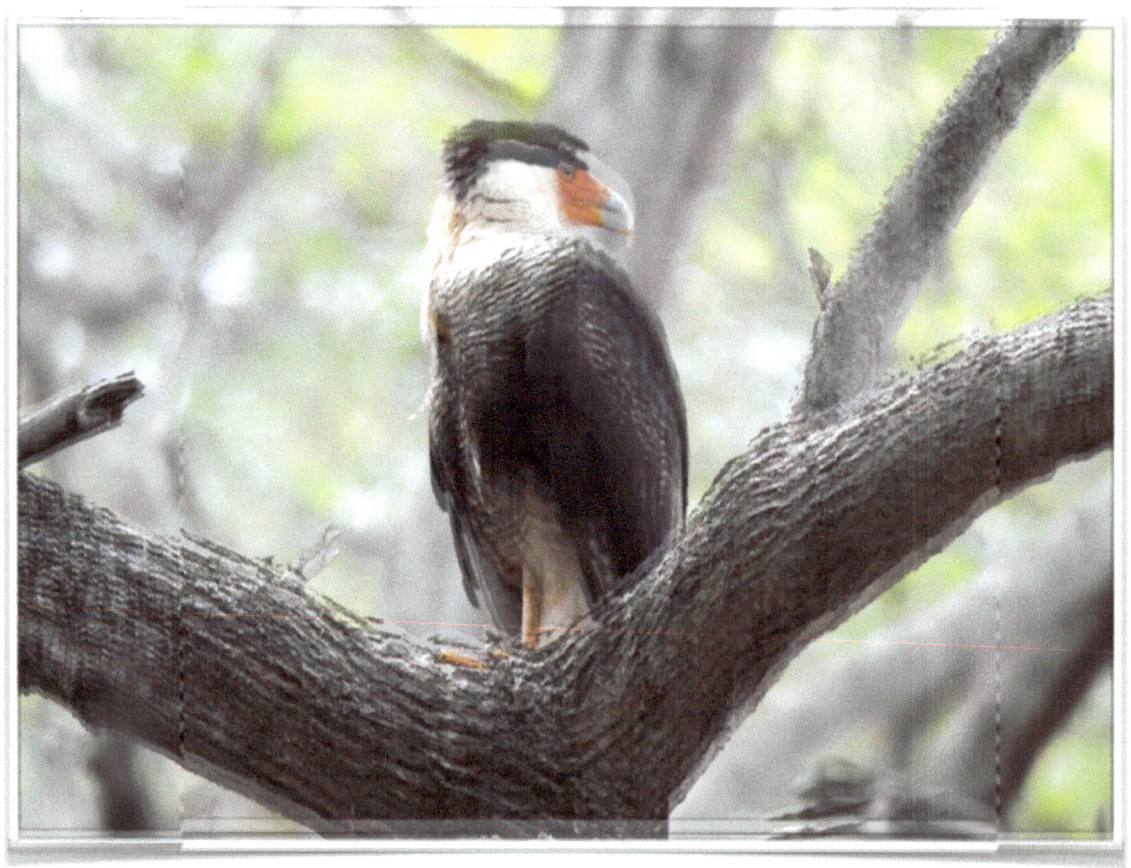

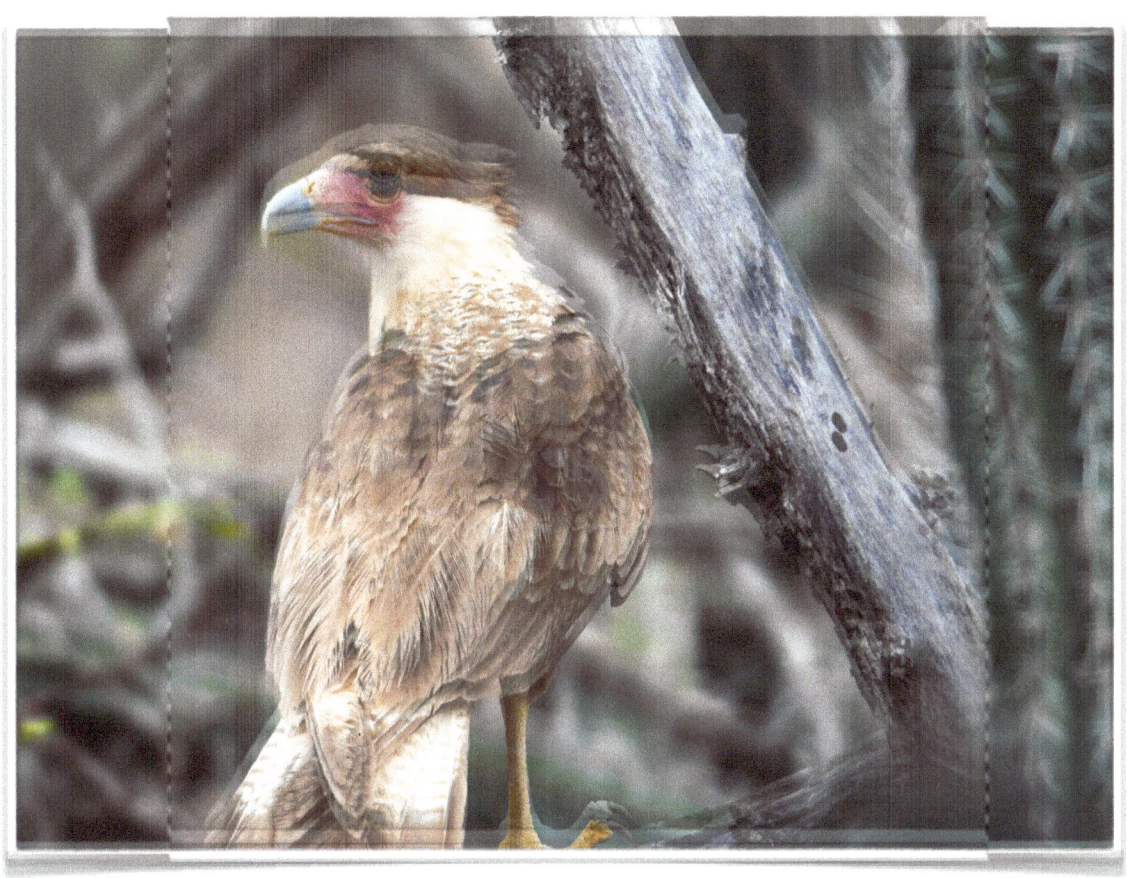
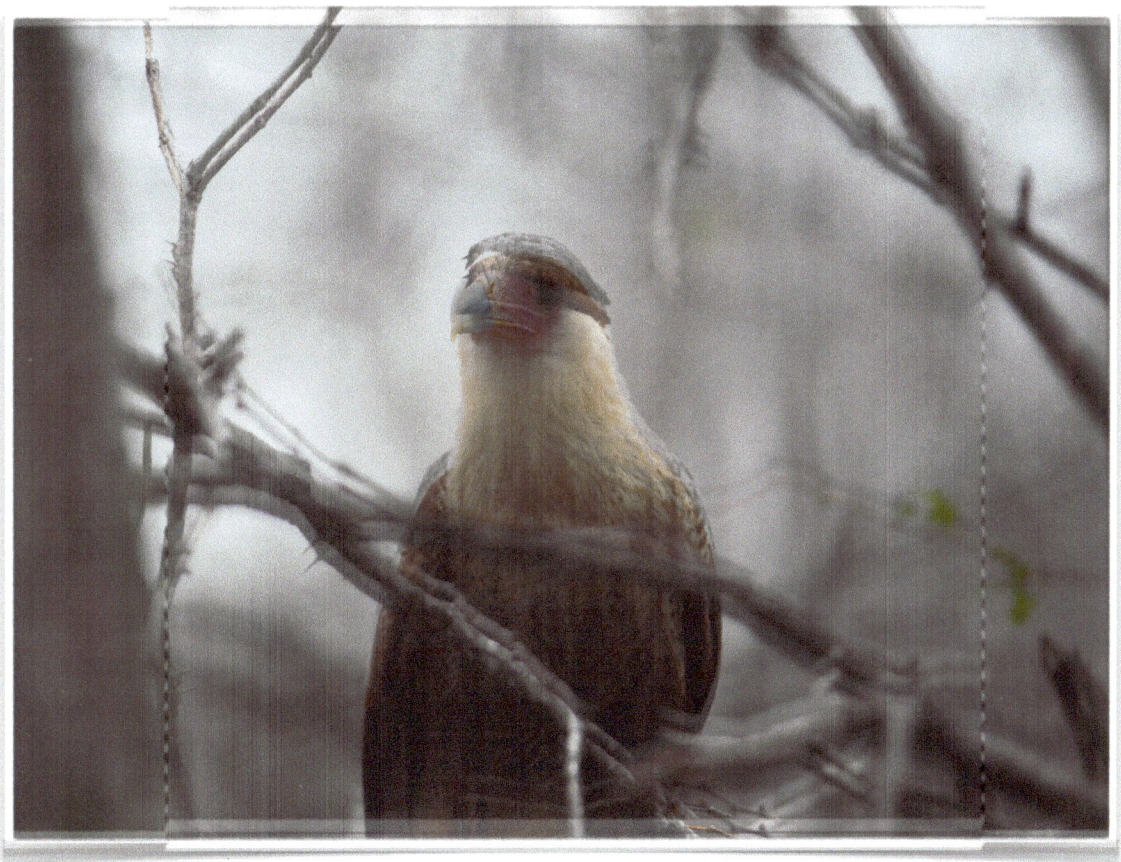

The Bananaquit

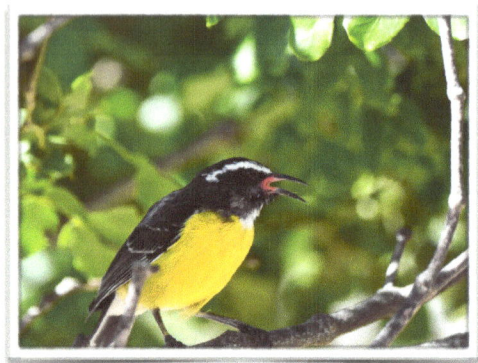

The Bananaquit is a dark grey bird with a yellow throat and it resembles a yellow warbler. It is very common in Bonaire, Aruba, Curacao and parts of the Caribbean region.

The bird can be found in open to semi-open habitats such as gardens and parks. It is sometimes referred to as the sugar bird due to its affinity for granular sugar in bowls or bird feeders.

The bananaquit mates year round and lays up to three eggs which are then incubated solely by the female.

All the photographs were taken by Norman Wei with his Nikon D500 camera and 500 mm prime lens in Bonaire and Aruba.

The Bananaquit

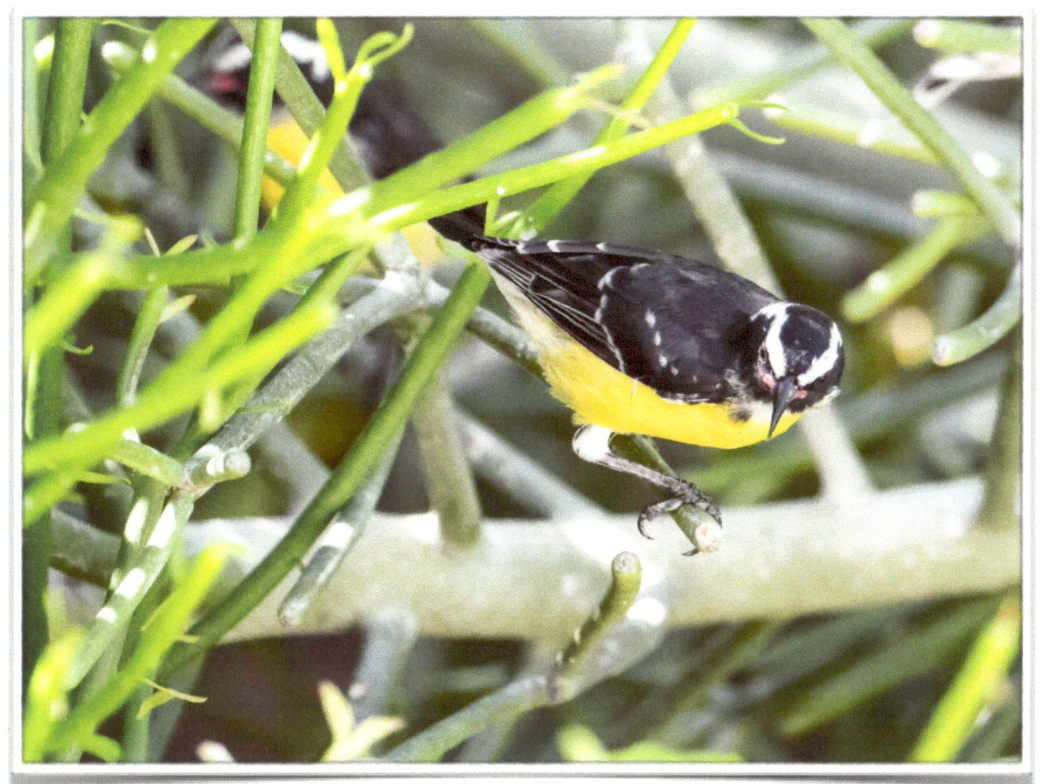

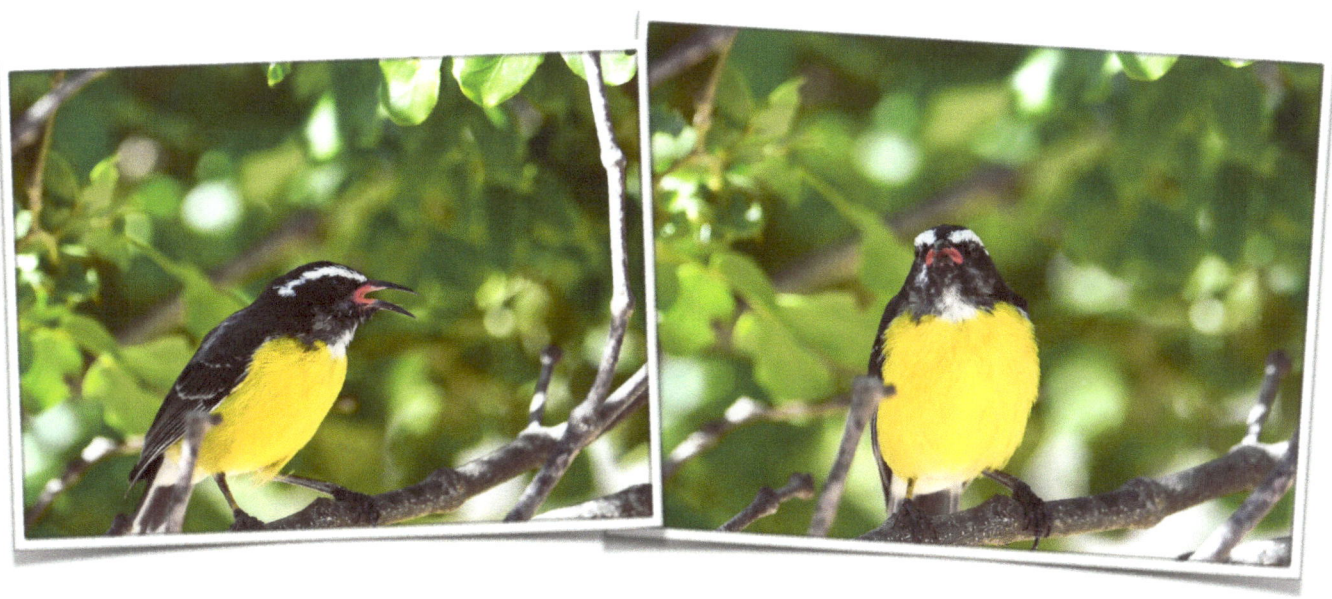

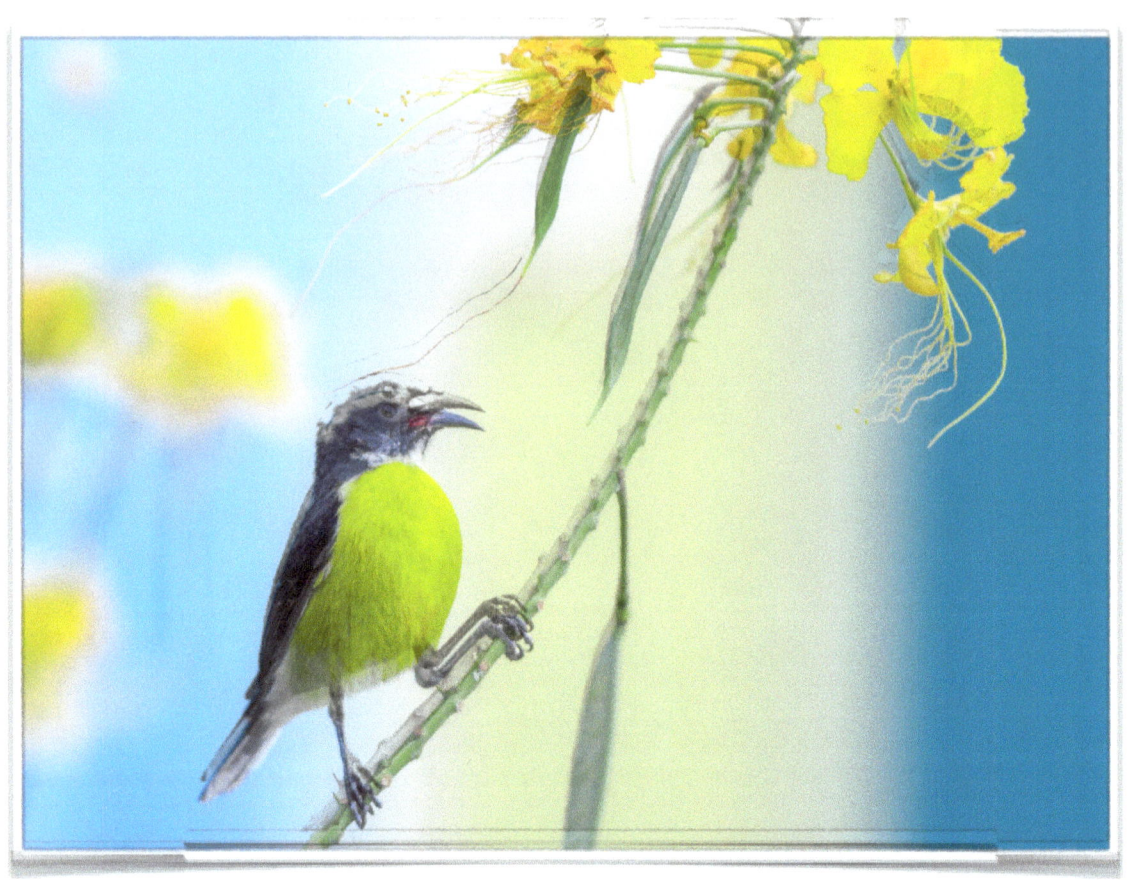
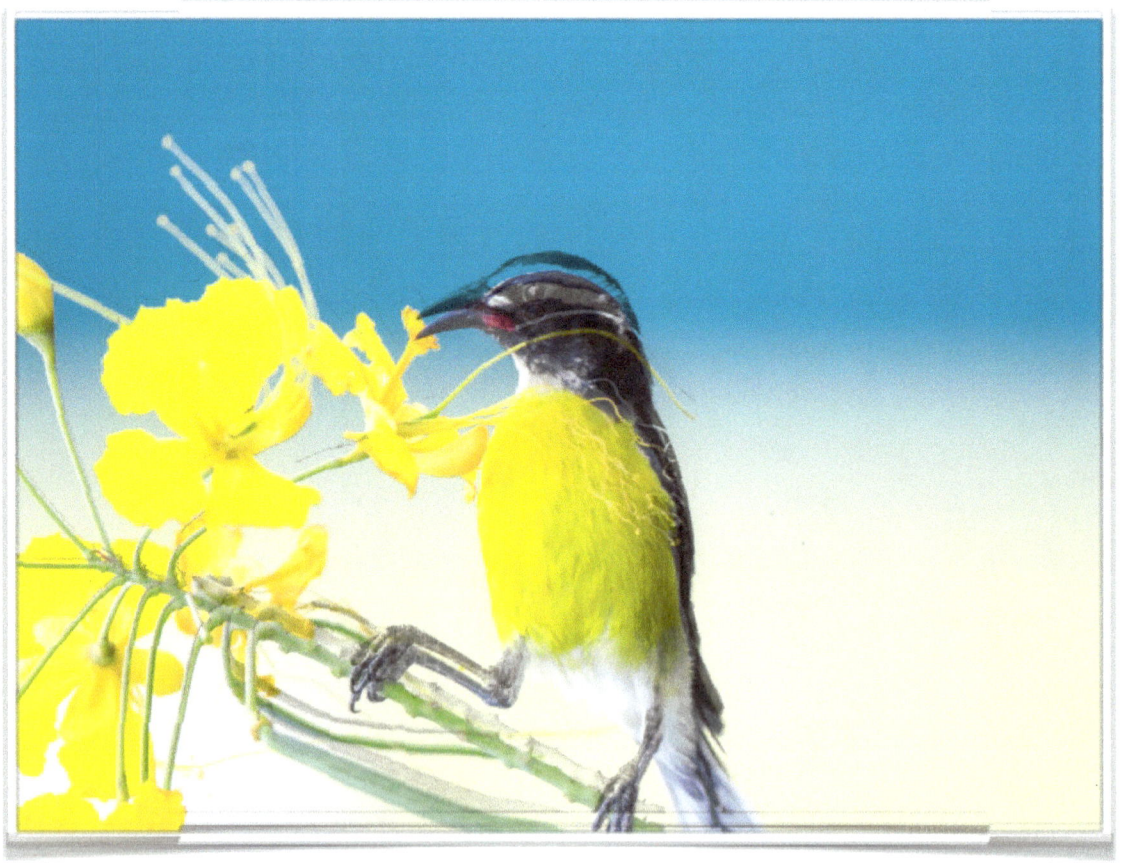

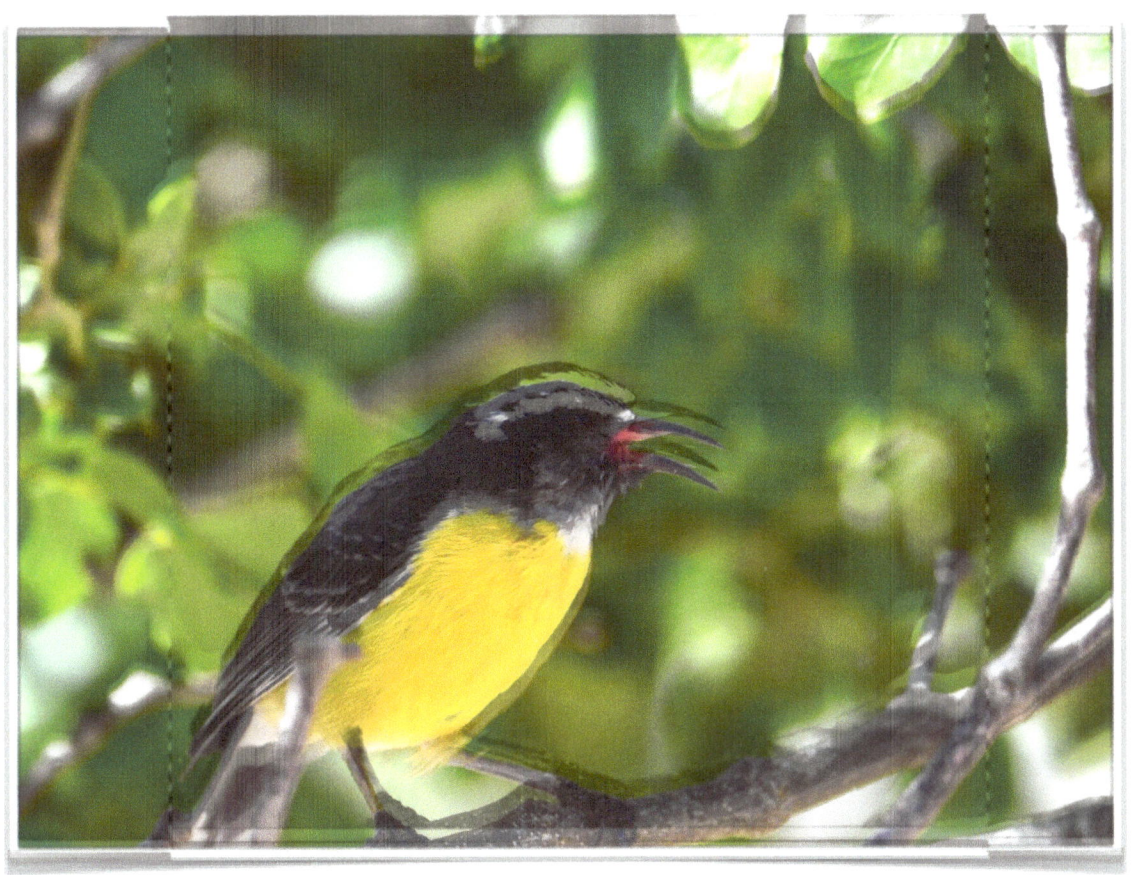

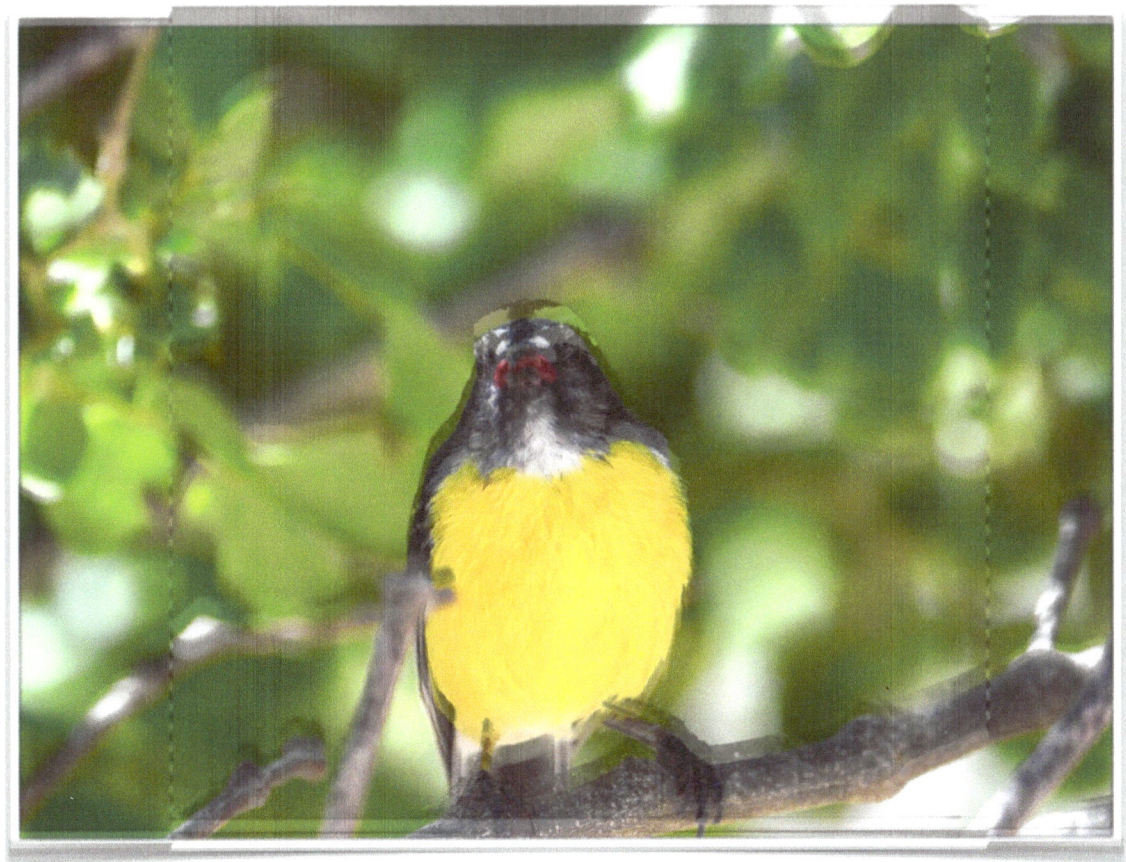

The Yellow-shouldered Amazon and other Parrots

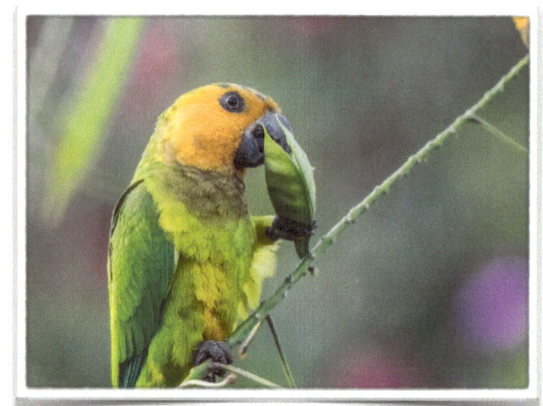

The Yellow-shouldered Amazon is a parrot found in Bonaire. It feeds on fruits, seeds and cactus flowers. Due to ongoing habitat loss, It was close to extinction at one time in Bonaire.

This birds make a very distinctive call that sounds like a rolling cur'r'k which can be heard easily by anyone in a car passing by.

They are very gregarious and like to form flocks of up to 100 birds

All the photographs of these parrots were taken by Norman Wei with his Nikon D500 camera and 500 mm prime lens in Bonaire.

The Yellow-shouldered Amazon

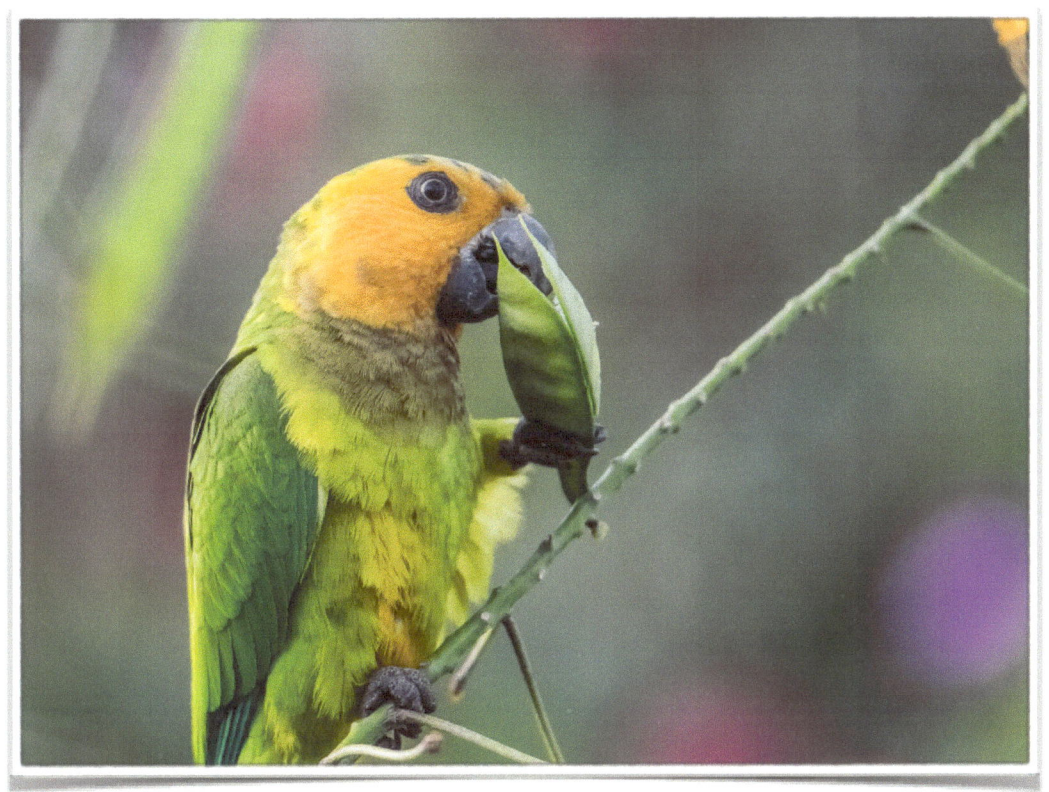

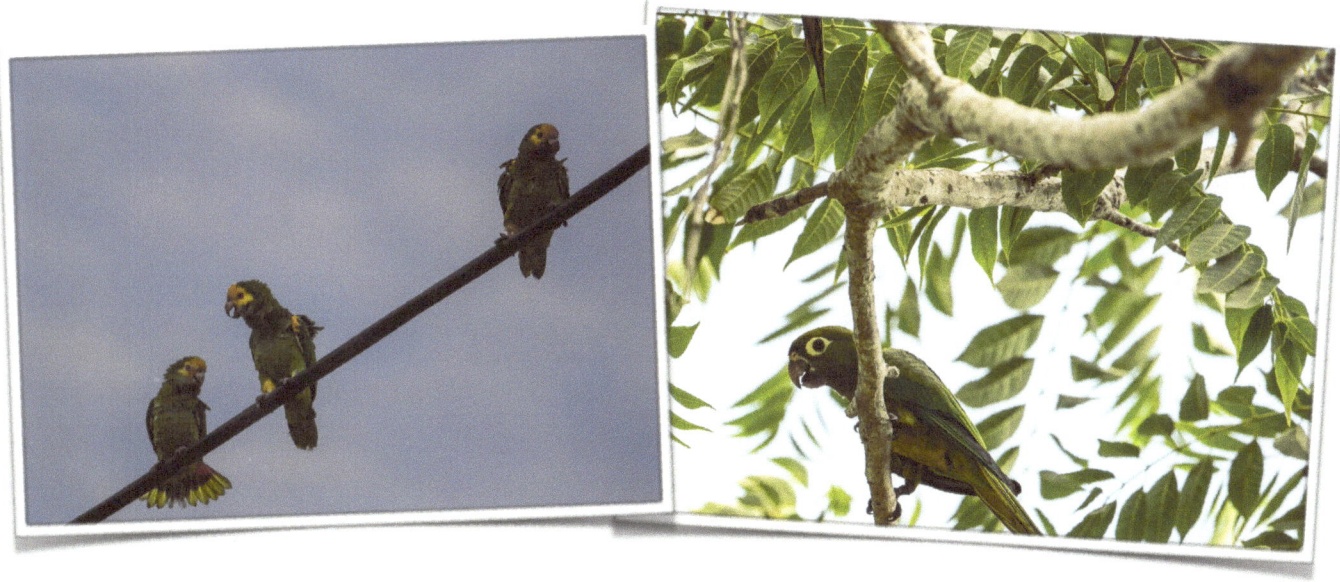

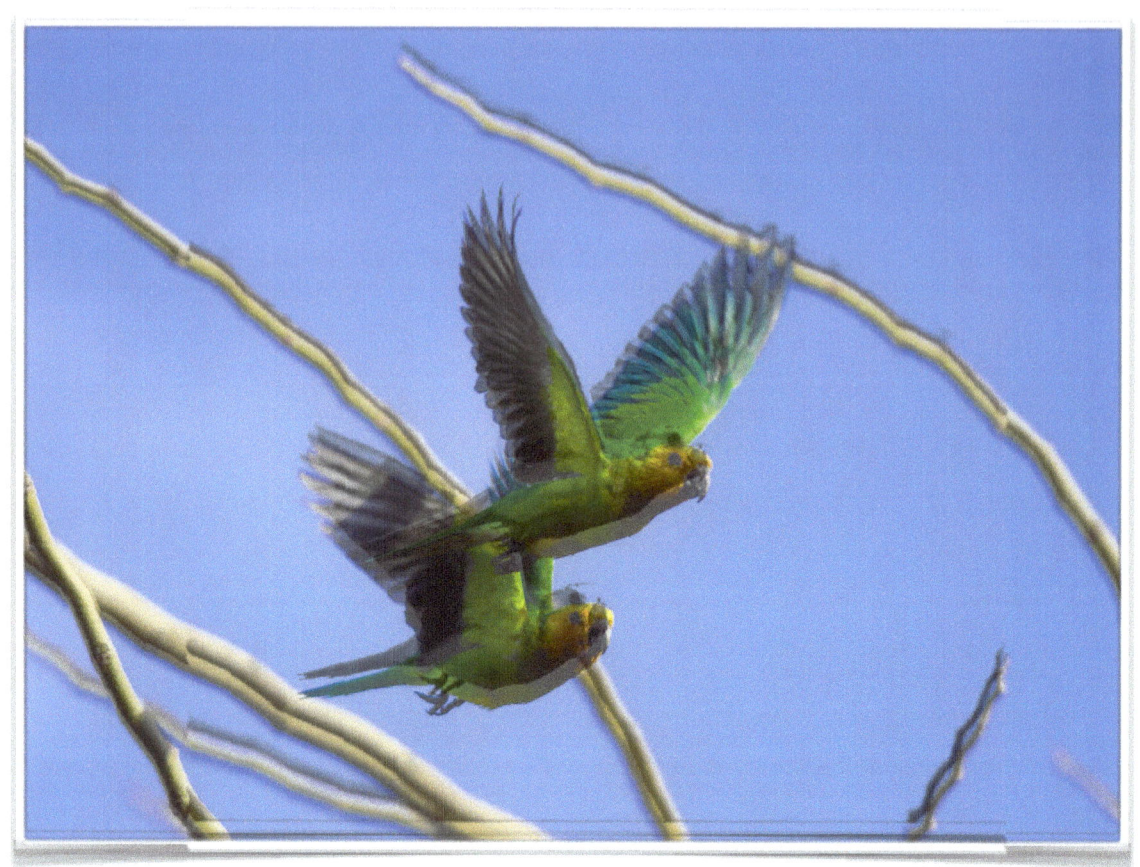
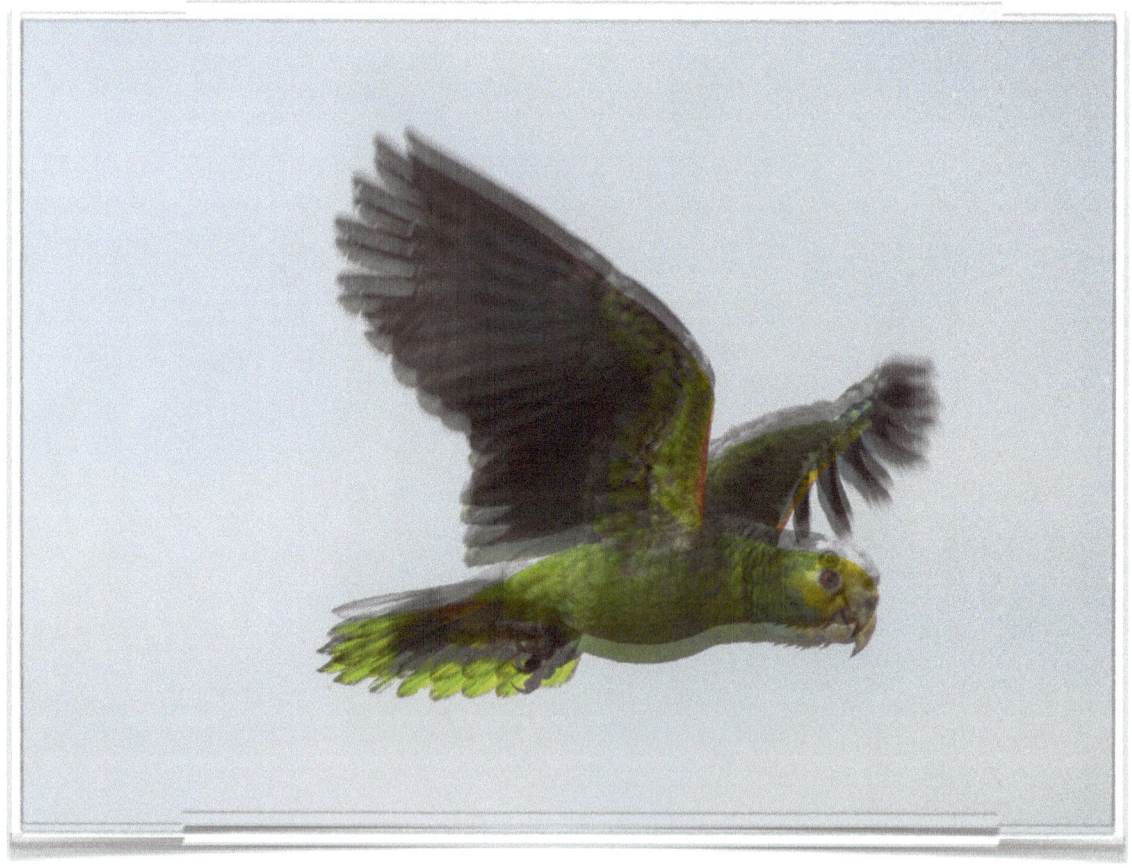

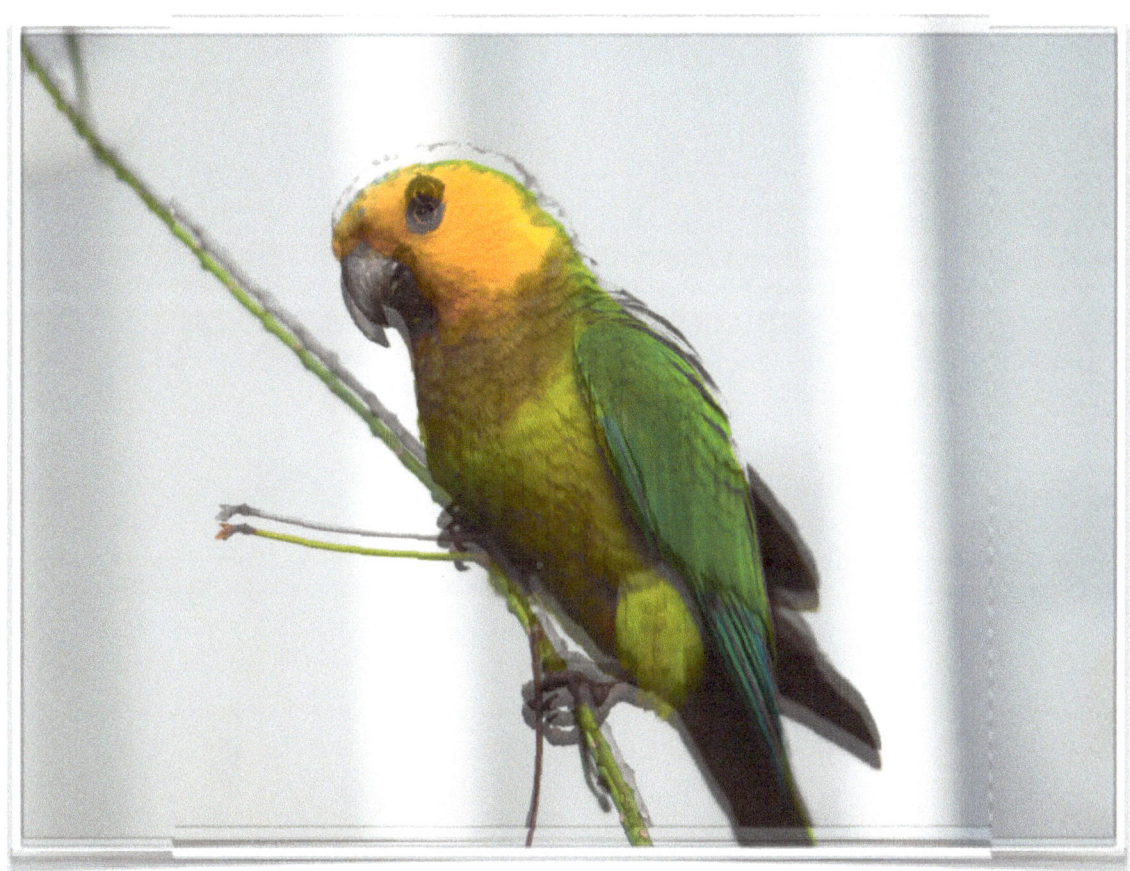
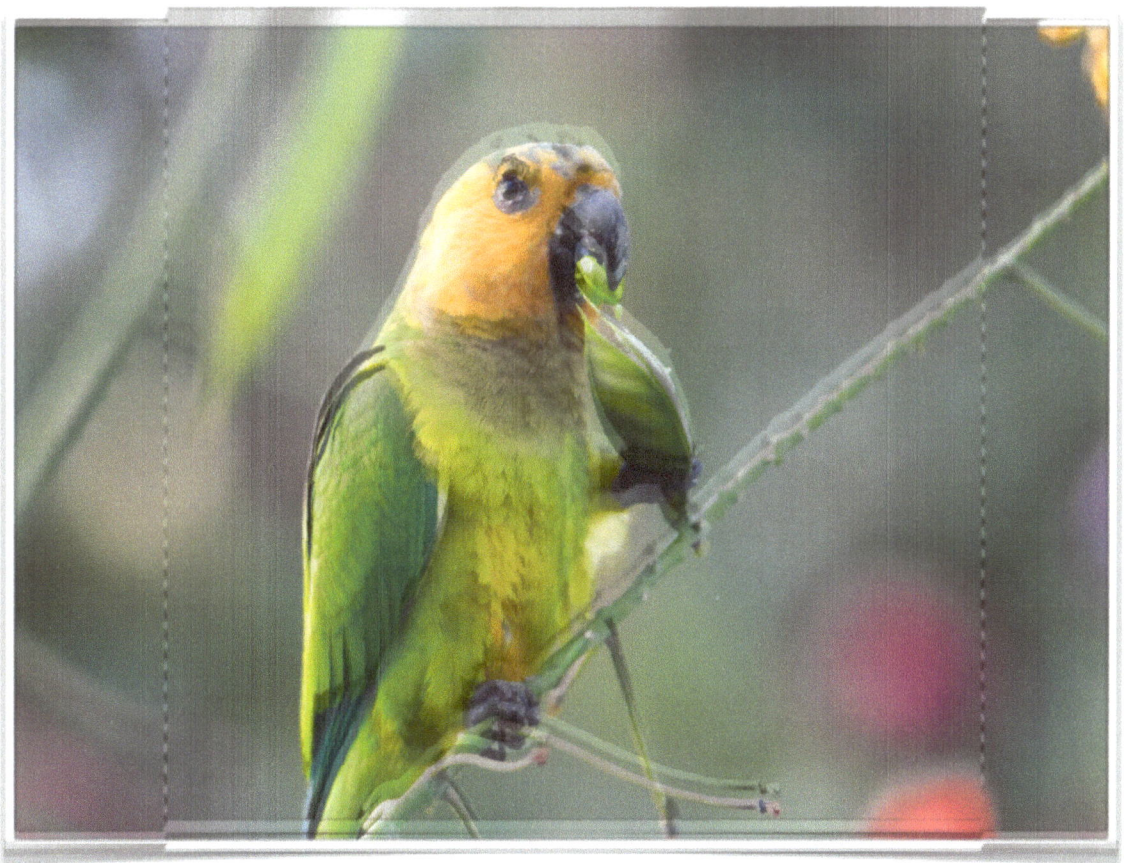

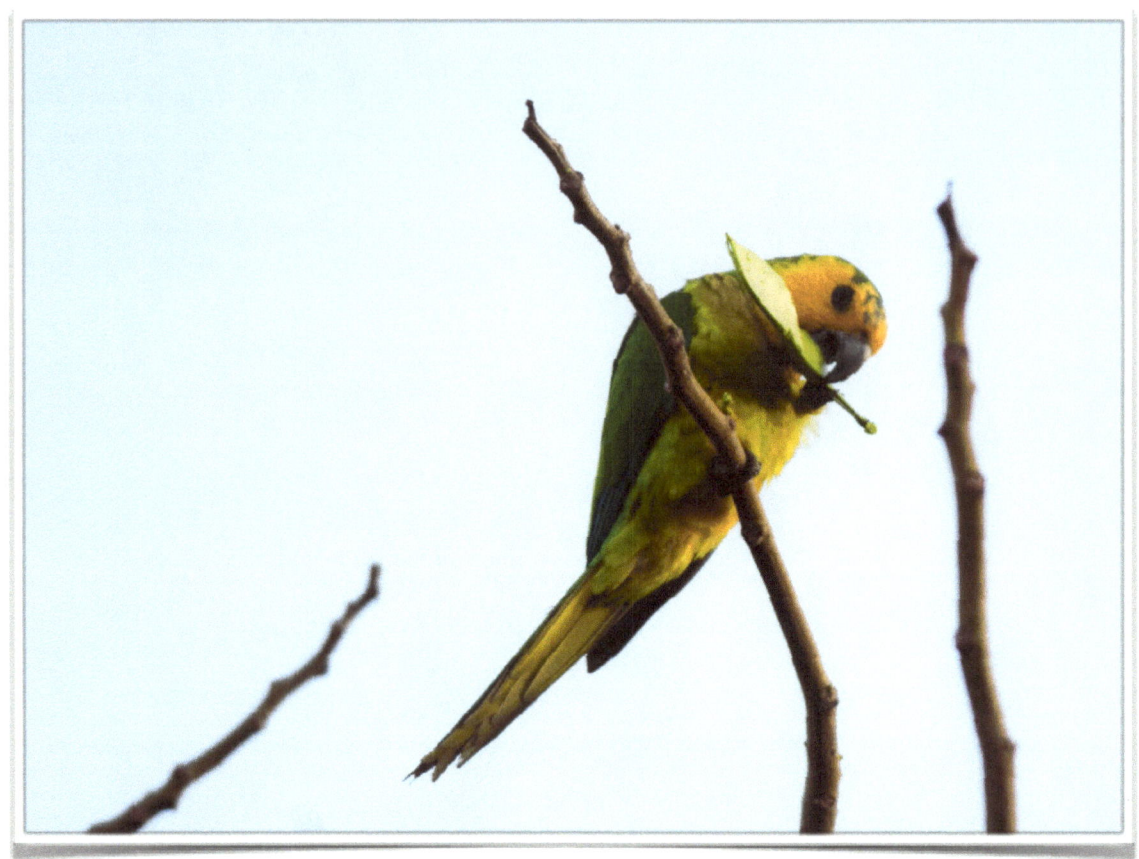
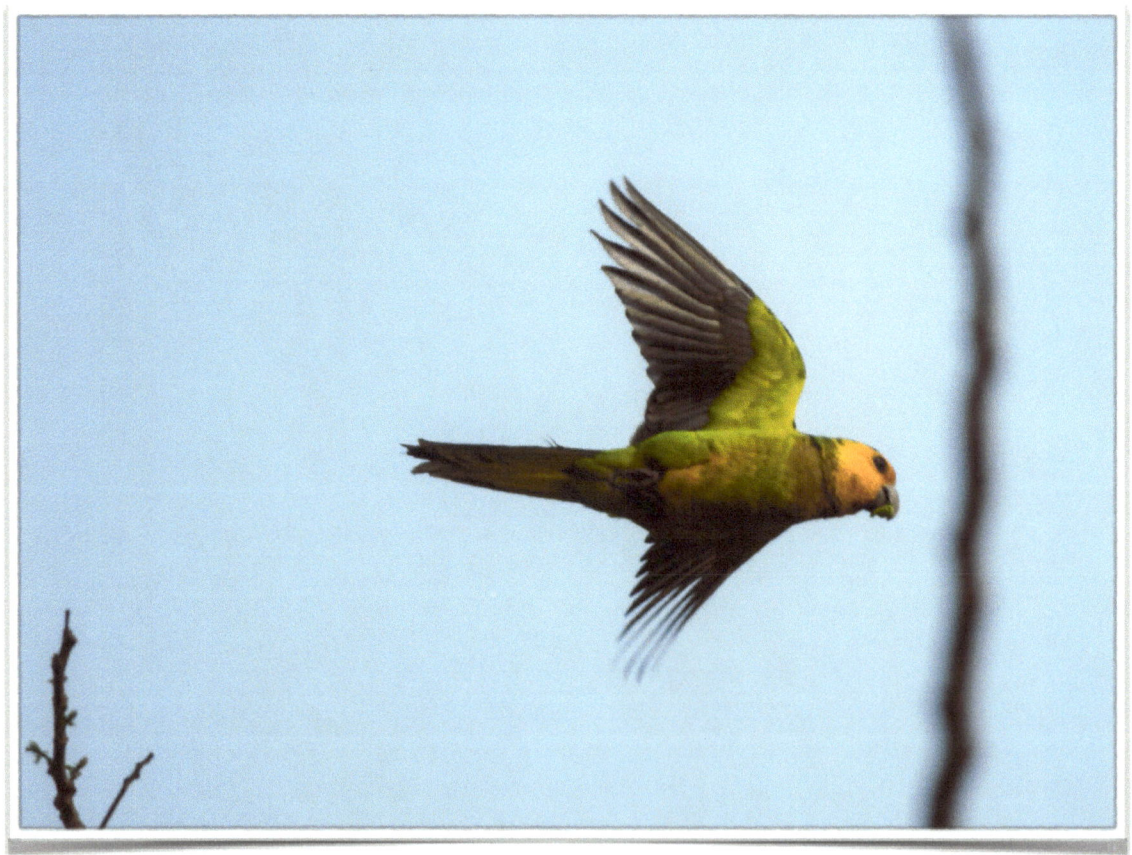

About the Photographer

Norman Wei is a nature photographer and environmental consultant who travels the world in search of exotic birds and wildlife.

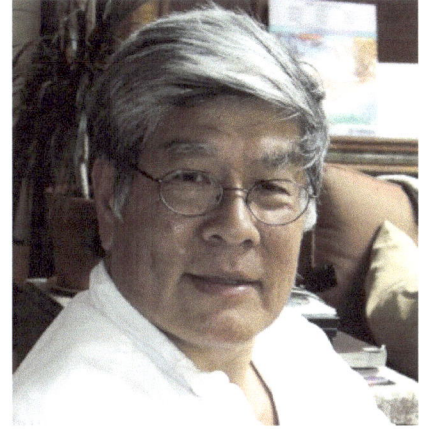

The photographs in this book were taken by him in Cozumel, Mexico and the Dutch Antilles Islands of Aruba, Bonaire and Curacao.

Prints and enlargements of Norman's photographs can be purchased at www.normanwei.smugmug.com. There are photographs of bald eagles, ospreys, pelicans, burrowing owls, hummingbirds, red-shouldered hawks, masked and brown boobies, magnificent frigatebirds, monk parakeets, painted buntings, bluejays, mockingbirds, great blue herons and many other birds on the website and more are added weekly.

Norman lives in Cape Coral, Florida with his lovely partner Cathy and several lovebirds. He is also active in scuba diving (underwater macrophotography), standup paddle boarding, kayaking, cycling and flying drones.

Norman can be reached at photos@normanwei.com.

Order photo prints at www.normanwei.smugmug.com.

This book is available at amazon.com and directly from Norman Wei. Cost is $15 with free shipping in the United States.

www.ingramcontent.com/pod-product-compliance
Lightning Source LLC
Chambersburg PA
CBHW051935210526
45473CB00006B/2261